WORLD SPICE
AT HOME

WORLD SPICE
AT HOME

New Flavors
for 75 Favorite Dishes

AMANDA BEVILL &
JULIE KRAMIS HEARNE

Photography by Charity Burggraaf

SASQUATCH BOOKS
SEATTLE

We would like to dedicate this book to our mothers. Their encouragement helped us to follow our passions in life. Cooking side by side with our moms and grandmothers has created lasting memories that are constantly being sparked by a familiar taste or smell. We hope this book will inspire you to gather with friends and family to cook, eat, and laugh together while building wonderful memories of food.

–AB & JKH

Printed in China

Published by Sasquatch Books

18 17 16 15 14   9 8 7 6 5 4 3 2 1

Editor: Gary Luke
Project editor: Em Gale
Photographs: Charity Burggraaf
Art Director: Anna Goldstein
Design: Joyce Hwang
Copy editor: Lisa Gordanier
Proofreader: Rachelle Longé McGhee

Library of Congress Cataloging-in-Publication Data is available.

ISBN: 978-1-57061-907-6

Sasquatch Books
1904 Third Avenue, Suite 710
Seattle, WA 98101
(206) 467-4300
www.sasquatchbooks.com
custserv@sasquatchbooks.com

Contents

Acknowledgments xi
Introduction: The Global Melting Pot of Spices 1
Spice Pantry 101: Tips, Tools & Techniques 3
Pure Spices 11
Spice Blends 23

SMALL BITES 57

SOUPS & STEWS 77

VEGETABLES & GRAINS 97

SHELLFISH & SEAFOOD 121

MEAT & POULTRY 149

SWEETS & BREADS 177

FINISHING TOUCHES 203

Index 221

Recipe List

SMALL BITES

Pogacha Flatbread with
  Sea Salt and Dukkah   59

Picadillo Peppers with Baharat   61

Lollapalooza Lamb Sliders with
  Berbere Ketchup   63

Besar Shrimp and Pineapple Skewers   67

Crostini with Dukkah-Encrusted
  Goat Cheese and Roasted Tomatoes   69

Irresistible Spiced Nuts   71

Za'atar Fries with Lemon-Pepper Aioli   73

Chinese Five-Spice Chicken Wings
  with Chili-Garlic Sauce   75

SOUPS & STEWS

Heirloom Tomato Gazpacho
  with Urfa Biber   79

Corn Chowder with Chanterelles,
  Bacon, and Za'atar   81

Crimson Beet and Apple
  Soup with Za'atar Cream   83

Golden Butternut Squash
  Soup with Besar   85

Creamy Cauliflower and Leek
  Soup with Tikka Masala   88

Sausage, White Bean, and Kale
  Soup with Besar   89

Udon Noodle Bowl with
  Prawns in Star Anise Broth   91

Spicy Chili with Berbere   92

Parsnip and Potato Soup
  with Poudre de Colombo   93

Fisherman's Stew with Harissa   95

VEGETABLES & GRAINS

Roasted Beet Salad with Watercress
  and Dukkah Goat Cheese   99

Crisp Oven-Roasted Broccoli with
  Lemon and Harissa   101

Summer Tomato Salad with Arugula
  and Urfa Biber   103

Bubble and Squeak
  with Poudre de Colombo   105

Vegetable Bread Salad with Za'atar   107

Honey-Glazed Eggplant
  with Ras el Hanout   109

Quinoa with Grilled Vegetables
and Kashmiri Dressing 112

Crispy Jicama and Watermelon
Salad with Sumac 114

Kale Tabbouleh with Pomegranate Seeds
and Ras el Hanout Dressing 117

Five-Seed Roasted Potatoes 118

Potato and Spinach Roll-Ups
with Poudre de Colombo 119

SHELLFISH & SEAFOOD

Dukkah-Encrusted Seared Scallops 123

Steamed True Cod
with Harissa-Garlic Sauce 125

Grilled Salmon with Za'atar
and Sauce Gribiche 127

Halibut Poached in Olive
Oil with Saffron 130

Dungeness Crab Melts
with Kashmiri Curry 133

Pan-Fried Sole with Berbere
and Lemon Butter 135

Coconut-Steamed Mussels
with Tikka Masala 137

Skillet Prawns
with Poudre de Colombo 138

Oyster Po' Boys with Harissa
and Muffuletta 141

Pan-Roasted Halibut
with Kashmiri Garam Masala Glaze 143

Shellfish Paella with Harissa
and Urfa Biber 145

Spicy Shrimp and Grits 147

MEAT & POULTRY

Seared Rib-Eye Steak with Baharat 151

Maple-Glazed Pork Chops with Besar 153

Pork Ribs with Chinese Five-Spice
and Barbecue Sauce 155

Pork Tenderloin with Ras el Hanout
and Urfa Biber Sweet Potatoes 158

Braised Beef Short Ribs with
Caramelized Onions and Baharat 161

Crusted Rack of Lamb
with Syrian Za'atar 163

Brisket with Berbere and Whiskey
Barbecue Sauce 165

Grilled Steak Salad
with Chinese Five-Spice 166

Baked Chicken with Tikka Masala Sauce 169

Melt-in-Your-Mouth Pot Roast
with Besar and Spaetzle 171

Oven-Roasted Chicken
with Harissa-Honey Glaze 173

Berbere Sloppy Joes 176

SWEETS & BREADS

Amanda's Cumin-Crusted Cornbread   179

Nectarine Upside-Down Cake with
  Cardamom Custard   181

Pumpkin Custard with Kashmiri
  Garam Masala and Maple Cream   184

Kashmiri Garam Masala–Infused
  Chocolate Truffles   186

Moist Carrot Cake
  with Kashmiri Garam Masala   189

Gingerbread Cake with Besar and
  Caramel Pears   191

Kashmiri Curry Bread Pudding
  with Spiced Nuts   193

Chinese Five-Spice Shortbread Cookies   194

Peach Cobbler with Nutmeg,
  Cardamom, and Cinnamon   197

Apple Galette with Chinese Five-Spice   198

Lavender Pavlovas with Blackberries
  and Cream   201

FINISHING TOUCHES

Sunshine Vinaigrette
  with Sumac and Aleppo   204

Apricot and Coriander Salad Dressing   205

Berbere Ketchup   207

Wirtabel's Melon Chutney   208

Turkish Sweet Onion Jam with Baharat   209

Ras el Hanout Spice Paste   211

Apple Butter with Ras el Hanout   212

Classic Harissa Paste   213

Spiced Rhubarb-Orange Marmalade   214

Chile-Infused Oil   217

Basic Curry Paste   218

Niter Kibbeh Spiced Butter   219

CHINESE FIVE-SPICE

BAHARAT

BESAR

BERBERE

DUKKAH

SYRIAN ZA'ATAR

KASHMIRI CURRY

ISRAELI ZA'ATAR

POUDRE DE COLOMBO

HARISSA

RAS EL HANOUT

TIKKA MASALA

KASHMIRI GARAM MASALA

Acknowledgments

To Julie for leading the way in this wonderful adventure in cooking and creativity. My heartfelt thanks and gratitude to James for eating and to Max for reading; I couldn't have done it without you. Special appreciation goes out to all my creative colleagues and customers at World Spice Merchants, most especially Holly, Robert, and Sherrie—thanks for making the spice magic happen.

—AMANDA BEVILL

To Amanda for opening up my world of spice and taking this journey of writing a book together. To my husband, Harker, and three boys, Reilly, Konrad, and Andrew, for expanding their tastes and willingness to try new things. To my mom, who is my mentor and my cheerleader, and to my dad for his ongoing support!

—JULIE KRAMIS HEARNE

We would like to thank everyone at Sasquatch Books—especially Gary Luke, our publisher. Thank you for believing in us and bringing this book to fruition. To Em Gale and Lisa Gordanier for their attention to detail. To Anna Goldstein and Joyce Hwang for their art direction and great vision, and to Charity Burggraaf for taking amazing photographs.

—AB & JKH

Introduction: The Global Melting Pot of Spices

Even before Europeans figured out that the world was round, they set sail looking for spices. Flavors had been trickling down the Silk Road for centuries, whetting their appetites. And as they sailed off toward the edge of the world, the global melting pot of spices really began to stir. Aromatic cloves and nutmeg emerged from the Spice Islands, mixed with black pepper and cardamom from India, cumin and coriander from Arabia, and then chiles from the Americas. Within the historical blink of an eye, spices once found only in a single, remote location became infused into the cuisines of every continent. Pepper once traded for a price above gold.

The lure of spices reaches beyond the flavoring of a dish in ways that remain as enticing today as they were centuries ago. The same temptation that launched thousands of trading ships from the docks still beckons, and it reaches us first and foremost through the nose. The sense of smell touches ancient triggers in the deep recesses of our brains, invoking emotions and memories without the intervening bother of thought. Spices are exotic, mysterious, and even sexy. One whiff can instantly transport you anywhere, from the spice bazaars of Morocco to the fields of lavender of Provence to the jungles of India. They evoke sensations of love at first sniff, and this is the essence that spices add to our food.

Take a peek inside your average spice pantry and you will likely find a lineup of the usual suspects—some of which may have been handed down a generation. All too often the spice pantry is a corner of the cabinet that only gets opened for a token pinch of this or that, and within it you'll find only a small fraction of the endless possibilities. Even adventurous cooks may find themselves with just one recipe for that special ingredient and are left wondering what to do with the rest. The jars stack up, unused.

Inspired by World Spice Merchants, this cookbook was designed to change that. Nestled below Pike Place Market on the Seattle waterfront, World Spice Merchants has been a hub of flavor explorations since 1995. It is a modern day spice bazaar representing a different kind of spice pantry—vibrant, diverse, and exploding with flavor; a pantry that changes with the seasons and is used so often the doors are always open. From any one of the hundreds of spices and blends on the shelves, we can create many dishes, making the flavor possibilities endless.

World Spice at Home is not intended to teach the art of any ethnic cuisine, though it does feature some of the most popular spice blends from around the world. The key to using spices easily in everyday cooking is to experiment and "cook outside the box." Who says you have to make curry with curry? Not us. Chinese five-spice is classically used to make Peking duck, but how about using it in cake or cookies, on pork tenderloin or spiced nuts, or even to add a kick to your next platter of chicken wings? Journey through the spice descriptions, tips, techniques, and recipes in this book and learn to use spices in everyday cooking with confidence, creativity, and ease. The possibilities are endless, and we will open the door to the world of spices and welcome you in.

Spice Pantry 101: Tips, Tools & Techniques

WHAT MAKES A SPICE A SPICE?

For all practical purposes, spices are aromatic bits of dried plant material used for seasoning food, and a host of familiar ingredients are called to mind at the use of the term. It reflects the common vernacular, as we typically refer to the "spice" pantry instead of the "spice, herb, salt, chile, and occasional dried vegetable" pantry. But the latter reveals the depth and diversity of what you'll find inside.

Spices are specifically defined as the non-leafy plant parts—seeds like cumin and coriander, barks like cinnamon, and berries like allspice. Roots and rhizomes like ginger and turmeric are also considered spices when dried.

Herbs are often combined with spices and have many of the same flavoring characteristics, but are a subset consisting of the green leafy parts of plants. They can be used fresh or dried, with different results. It is true that some fresh flavors are lost as an herb is dried, but the ones that remain are more concentrated—offering a distinctly different flavor profile. Chiles are another large subcategory within the pantry. Chiles are fruits and they come in a staggering array of shapes and flavors. Beyond these you will find an increasingly eccentric cast of characters within the spice world, from sweet-smelling flowers like roses and lavender to asafoetida, the resin of the giant Middle Eastern fennel bulb that has a dubious aroma until it is cooked.

The unifying theme across this botanical collection is that these aromatic and pungent ingredients can compel the senses and transform your food from ordinary to extraordinary. That is what makes a spice a spice.

SPICE QUALITY & FRESHNESS

Quality and freshness are one and the same when it comes to spices. Look for spices in whole form whenever possible; they should be vibrant in appearance and color, not dull or faded. It's not always possible to smell or taste before purchase, but if it is, the smell should be strong and pungent. If you can identify clear nuances in the aroma, even better.

The word *freshness* can be ambiguous when it comes to spices, because they technically have a longer shelf life than many food products. However, spices do lose flavor over time, so buy in small amounts and replenish as needed. It also helps to buy your spices as close to the source as you can to ensure that they haven't been stored for too long before you take them home. Artisan shops specializing in spices typically have a fresher supply than grocery outlets or warehouse stores.

SPICE STORAGE, SHELF LIFE & SEASONAL ROTATION

Spices should never be kept longer than a year, and sometimes that is too long. This general guideline is based on the harvest cycle of plants and the seasonal nature of our cooking: if you harvest once a year, discard the old spices when the new crop arrives. As spices age, they don't really "go bad," they just kind of fade away . . . and some fade faster than others. Resist the temptation to simply use more of an older spice to compensate for its age. The flavors that are lost as spices age alter the ones that remain.

From a practical standpoint, we recommend overhauling the spice cabinet twice each year, at the changing of the seasons. Once in the fall, to get fresh flavors for winter squash and pumpkins, cold weather comfort foods, and holiday baking; then again in the spring, as we anxiously await the first shoots of green vegetables and impatiently dust off the barbecue grill. Each time you buy fresh, vibrant spices, discard the faded ones from the season before.

For maximum freshness and shelf life, always store your spices in nonreactive, airtight containers, away from heat and light. This will prevent all those luscious flavors and aromas from slipping away. Not all spices are created equal when it comes to shelf life. Aromatics like nutmeg and cardamom lose flavor more quickly, whereas resinous spices like paprika and turmeric are more stable.

TO GRIND OR NOT TO GRIND

The reason to grind your own spices is simple: the process brings out flavors you can't get any other way. The difference is striking when you smell a freshly ground spice compared to one ground even a few weeks before. Both are aromatic, but the flavors begin to dissipate as soon as a spice is ground. Grinding your own spices is worth the effort! It also gives you an opportunity to create different textures to use in your cooking. You can grind finely for sprinkling on salads, medium for adding to soups and braises, or coarse for rubbing meats.

Best-case scenario?

Whenever possible, buy whole spices and grind them right before use. The best all-purpose tool for taking spices from whole form into powder is an electric spice or coffee grinder with a strong motor and blades. We recommend both Krups and KitchenAid. It is a good idea to have one grinder that is dedicated only to spices—because curry and coffee is *not* a good flavor combination, especially first thing in the morning.

Here are a some tips on using an electric mill:

• When grinding whole spices into powder, it can be helpful to start with a little bit more spice in the grinder than you will ultimately need. This is because even the best electric mills cannot always grind everything completely. You will sometimes be left with pieces to sift out through a fine mesh sieve. The excess can be returned to your spice jar and stored until the next use.

• Spice blends consist of multiple ingredients that may settle into layers within your storage jar, and it is important to get a good mix of ingredients before grinding. For this reason, we like to store our blends in wide-mouthed jars so that a spoon can easily reach in and remix the contents before scooping some out to grind.

• In between uses, grind rice or bread crumbs to pick up and remove any residual spices, then discard. Wipe out the grinder with a dry cloth to clean further.

• A mortar and pestle is another essential tool for working with spices. They come in a variety of shapes, sizes, and textures, and are perfect for cracking and breaking small bits of spice and for turning powders into pastes. They are also great for coarse-cracking peppercorns or other seeds for a variety of textures to include in crusts and rubs. Larger and harder spices, like star anise and cloves, should be cracked in a mortar and pestle before grinding. This makes them easier to grind and prevents the larger pieces from getting stuck below the blades.

Sometimes using preground spices is the best and only option. Some spices, like paprika and turmeric, are only available preground. And there are even times when grinding your own spices isn't practical. As long as they are fresh, the flavors will carry through in your dish.

TOASTING WHOLE SPICES

Toasting whole spices will enhance their flavors even more, and it is easy to do. Preheat a dry, heavy skillet over medium heat, and then add the whole spices. It doesn't matter if the skillet is too big—that just gives more room for the spices to move around. When you smell the spices beginning to toast, shake the pan back and forth to evenly toast all sides. This typically takes only a few minutes. Remove the pan from the heat when the toasting is uniform but before the spices begin to smoke. Transfer the spices to a bowl or tray to cool right away.

Some whole spices can be toasted together—like cumin, coriander, and black peppercorns. This is helpful because you can gauge doneness by the lighter-colored spices like coriander (where you can easily see the browning occur), whereas with black peppercorns, it is harder to see a change of color. Oilier spices like cinnamon, cloves, and cardamom toast more quickly and are best toasted separately from less oily ones.

MAKING A PASTE WITH SPICES

Making pastes is a great way to really utilize your spices. Any spice blend can be used to make a paste, and it may be combined with a range of fresh ingredients to create a rainbow of flavors. Pastes usually consist of dried spices, fresh ingredients, and a little liquid. They may be used as condiments, glazes, wet rubs, or as a base for soups, stews, and curries. The basic steps to make a paste are quick and easy. First, chop or slice the fresh ingredients into manageable sizes, then combine them with the spices and a little liquid in a mortar bowl. Then the real fun begins! Use the pestle to smash the ingredients together to the desired consistency.

If you are making a larger volume, a food processor or even a handheld immersion blender can be a time saver, but be sure to pulse it gently to keep the consistency of a paste rather than liquefying the mixture.

TURNING A SPICE BLEND INTO A DRY RUB

Spice rubs are a remarkable way to season any cut of meat—from a quick, weeknight tenderloin to a slow-cooked pulled pork shoulder or brisket—they form a flavorful crust in combination with the natural juices from meat as it cooks. And the good news is that there is more to rubs than barbecue! Try our Seared Rib-Eye Steak with Baharat (page 151) or Maple-Glazed Pork Chops with Besar (page 153). The flavor possibilities are limited only by your imagination and pantry options.

Rubs consist of a mixture of spices, often combined with sugar and salt, and typically have a slightly coarse texture. You can dust a dry rub on lightly for subtle seasoning or go with a heavy hand for bold flavor. Rubs don't need to be applied in a very precise quantity—simply smear some on, shake off the excess, and approximate the perfect amount. We recommend going lighter on fish, medium on chicken and pork, and heavier on things that cook for a long time, such as brisket or a large roast.

Making your own rubs at home increases the versatility of your spice pantry without taking up any more precious shelf space. Start with a simple 3:2:1 ratio: 3 parts spices, 2 parts sugar, and 1 part salt. Brown sugar and kosher salt are standard, all-purpose additions, but in a pinch just use what you have. The brown sugar offers its characteristic deep color and flavor, and kosher salt has a good texture. You can vary the proportions according to your tastes. We also love to add fresh herbs and citrus zest to brighten the natural flavors of fish, pork, or chicken.

Rubs can be applied right before you slide something into the oven, or an hour or two ahead to allow the flavors to penetrate more deeply. Both methods yield great flavor.

SPICE INFUSIONS: USING LIQUIDS TO DRAW OUT & ENHANCE FLAVORS

A simple way to transfer the flavor of almost any spice is to infuse it into an oil, butter, or liquid. The infusion can then be used in a wide variety of ways to disperse the flavors into your food. When making an infusion, use whole or coarsely ground spices because they are usually strained out before use, and finely ground powders are difficult to remove. Some infusions are gently heated to help extract the properties of the spices and some are left to steep for a period of time. The results can be both colorful and flavorful.

Spice-infused oil or butter can be kept on hand for use in cooking and at the table. Chile-infused oils are wonderful because they allow you to add a very controlled amount of heat to any dish, and spiced butters can add powerful seasoning to just about anything. It isn't always necessary to remove chiles or whole spices from an infused oil, and the beauty of the pods bobbing in the oil adds a homey touch.

Spices can also be infused into milk or cream over low heat; the longer they steep in the liquid, the more intense the flavor. This technique is classically used in custards, ice cream bases, chocolate ganache, and other desserts. Star anise, cardamom, vanilla bean, cinnamon, and cloves are often used this way.

You can also infuse whole spices into a sugar-water solution (using equal amounts of both) to make a simple syrup. Add whole spices like star anise, cinnamon, cloves, and even orange peel, and bring to a boil. Remove from the heat and allow to steep for fifteen minutes or longer. Cool and strain, then add to sparkling water, hot water, or alcohol. We even like to add a little to whipping cream instead of sugar.

Alcohol infusions have a reserved seat at happy hour! Mulled wine and sangria are centuries-old recipes and are delightful examples of the joys of combining spices with wine. Spices can also be infused into whiskey or spirits for creative cocktails year-round.

Vinegar is very effective at extracting flavor from spices, and keeping vinegar infusions on hand for use in marinades and vinaigrettes is a handy seasoning shortcut. Heat isn't necessary or recommended for vinegar infusions. Simply add whole or cracked spices to your vinegar and allow the flavors to emerge. Our favorite choice for infusing is apple cider vinegar.

HOW TO KNOW WHEN TO ADD SPICES

Spices can be added to a dish at different times, from the earliest stages of a long, slow braise to the final garnish at the table. For many dishes, you will add seasoning more than once, as you would with salt. Starting small is the best approach.

With slow-cooked meals like soups and stews, create layers of flavor by adding spices two or three times during cooking. First, early on when you initially heat your oil in the pan, so the flavors can infuse into the oil; again when you assemble everything in the pot; and toward the end of cooking, as a finishing touch. This approach will allow deep flavors to develop from the spices used early on and also add back the vibrant high notes at the finish that may have been lost in the longer cooking time.

USING SPICES WITH CONFIDENCE, CREATIVITY & EASE

Keep Your Spice Pantry Fresh

It is easier to take a creative leap in your cooking if you don't have to run out to the market every time you need a few teaspoons of a certain spice. Many notable meals spring from a dish made with what's on hand, so make sure you've got plenty of spices to work with.

Trust your nose

For years we've been guiding spice enthusiasts with a simple motto: "If you like the way it smells, you'll like the way it tastes." So go ahead, give it a try.

Keep simple synergies in mind

It is easy to expand the range of flavors in your recipe box by taking one great combination and expanding on it. For example, curries work well with squash. So try a curry blend with baked squash, squash soup, and any other squash recipes.

Take it somewhere new

- Turn a spice blend into a meat rub
- Add spices to baked goods
- Try spice blends in salad dressings

Pure Spices

Pure spices can be used alone or in combination to season your food, providing a subtle accent or bold flavors to a dish. Pure spices can also be used to modify a favorite spice blend by adding something new to the mix. Just one spice can be used to increase the heat or sweetness of a blend, or add a desired savory note to a dish.

The pure spices in this glossary are all components of the featured spice blends in this book—and they add layers of flavor in the recipes that follow. Some are familiar and often used, like black peppercorns, cumin, and coriander. Others, like ajwain and long pepper, are exotic and contribute a special dash of taste. This glossary will teach you about the intricacies of flavor, whether you stock your pantry with pure spices and make your own blends or purchase blends premade.

AJWAIN SEED

The intriguing aroma of ajwain is similar to cumin and also contains some of the same flavor compounds as the herb, thyme. Common in both Indian and African cuisines, this unusual seed spice can be used whole for pops of flavor or ground to distribute seasoning into a dish. Experiment using it in place of cumin, but with a lighter hand. The strong flavors of ajwain can easily overpower a dish. You'll find it in our berbere and ras el hanout blends for a flavorful twist.

ALLSPICE

As the name implies, allspice imparts several distinct flavors, including those of cinnamon, nutmeg, clove, and pepper. This wonderfully versatile spice is at home in much more than pumpkin pie and gingerbread. Native to Central America, it is an essential ingredient in Caribbean cuisine as well as a key component of both berbere and baharat. We recommend buying the whole dried berries and grinding them fresh.

ANISE SEED

These tiny seeds impart sweet accents and a light licorice bouquet. We use them to contrast the sour sumac in Syrian za'atar and complement the savory aspects of ras el hanout. Anise seed is a signature flavor in biscotti.

BAY LEAF, TURKISH

Drop a bay leaf into your soup or stew when it's time to simmer; you will be rewarded with a deep savory flavor base and a balanced bit of bitter alongside notes of camphor and pine. This is an herb that is most often used dry—and almost always infused and then discarded—but the creative cook can crumble one into a spice mix to enjoy the same results.

CARAWAY SEED

These seeds have a deeply intense savory character that is best used in a supporting role to other spices so as not to overpower a dish—unless, of course, you are making rye bread, which boasts caraway as a singular flavor. We use it in our harissa and ras el hanout to round out their flavor profiles.

CARDAMOM SEED & POD

Native to India, cardamom plants thrive in the jungle understory. The potent essential oils release an intense bouquet of floral and camphor notes—you know you have fresh cardamom when your eyes water as you lean in for a whiff! The bright green pods are used for infusions and for flavoring rice or grain dishes, but are always removed before serving. Crack them in a mortar and pestle before using to help release the flavors. The small, gray-black seeds are easy to grind and can be used for baking. Cardamom provides vital aromatic flavor to spices blends of all types and is the signature note in the *chai masalas* of India.

CHAMOMILE

Chamomile is more commonly found on the tea shelf instead of in the spice pantry, but we like to keep a little on hand for a top note in our ras el hanout. The aroma of freshly cut hay and a hint of bittersweet undertones are subtle contributions to the blend. The added bonus is that we can always have a relaxing cup of tea on hand as well.

CHILES

Chiles have been cultivated for centuries into more varieties than any other seasoning. Many countries and cultures have a signature chile, like paprika from Hungary and the appellation-controlled *piment d'Espelette* from France. Once native only to the Americas, these fiery, flavorful fruits have made their way into kitchens worldwide.

You don't have to love super-hot food to appreciate chiles. There is an enormous range of heat level and flavor to be explored to find the one for you—from the terrifying ghost chile (hottest in the world) to the mildest paprika that barely makes its way onto the heat chart. We recommend keeping a few varieties in the pantry to cover a range of uses and heat levels.

Aleppo Pepper

This delightfully mild chile from Syria is like sunshine in a jar. Unlike the straightforward heat of cayenne or other sharp, hot chiles, Aleppo pepper offers a warm handshake followed by a hint of citrus. The best way to appreciate the nuances of Aleppo is when it is used alone or in a simple combination. Next time you want to flavor a dish with "just pepper," try using "just Aleppo." Aleppo can be easily infused in oil and kept on hand for cooking or for offering at the table for dipping. Available only in flake form, this chile should appear slightly moist and sticky. The color can range from brick to bright red.

Cayenne Pepper

If you need simple heat without a lot of distinctive flavor, this red-hot chile does the trick. There is a range of heat levels available from varieties originating in India, Africa, and beyond. Cayenne is usually sold preground and is easily mixed into homemade spice blends.

Guajillo Chile

Guajillo is favored at World Spice Merchants for its deep flavor and versatility. It is the perfect base chile for hearty blends and the ideal mild chile accent wherever one is needed. A signature flavor in enchiladas and Tex-Mex cuisine, guajillos are equally at home in everything from besar to curries to harissa. These mild- to medium-heat chiles are available whole or in flake form and should have a dark, rich color. Pliability is a good sign that they are fresh.

Hungarian Paprika

This familiar spice is often underutilized merely as a colorful topping, but a more generous measure is what you need to make a strong base for spice blends like harissa and berbere. The Hungarian variety is our go-to choice.

Pequin Chile

Hot red pequin chiles are a favorite because they are small and mix easily into blends without having to be cut into smaller bits first. If you want to add whole chiles to a spice blend that will be ground before use, these are a good choice. Their flavor is strong, bright, and *hot*.

Smoked Paprika

A culinary invention from Spain, the addition of smoked paprika to your spice cabinet will give you the ability to add a rich chile base and authentic smoky flavor to any dish without adding heat—a culinary magic trick! While it is available *picante* (hot) and *agrodulce* (bittersweet), the most versatile is the *dulce* (sweet) variety. Be sure to purchase authentic Spanish smoked paprika—not imitation products with artificial smoke flavor. Consider substituting a smaller amount of smoked paprika in any recipe that calls for the standard variety—it will offer a new dimension to your next plate of deviled eggs!

Urfa Biber

Rich, raisiny, smoky, coffee goodness: that is the flavor of urfa biber. Accent those qualities with a mild warmth that builds as you eat it, and urfa wins the Most Sultry Spice award, hands down. The dark, rich flavors are formed by "sweating" the urfa biber chiles as they dry. A staple in Turkish cuisine, urfa is used to season meats, kebabs, and all manner of dips, sauces, and spreads. The large, moist, and chewy flakes don't require cooking to release their magic, and they're much more palatable than the average raw chile flake. Let your creativity run wild with this one—especially with desserts, since urfa biber works well paired with caramel, all forms of chocolate, and fruits like strawberries and bananas.

CINNAMON

The warm, pungent aroma and flavor of cinnamon is so familiar and beloved that it requires little elaboration. The most common cinnamon on the American market is cassia cinnamon from Indonesia, and the popularity of this spice in our cuisine keeps a fresh supply flowing our way. Cassia cinnamon from Vietnam is also becoming more available and is worth the effort to find; its distinctive oil composition makes it more intense than the Indonesian variety. Cassia cinnamon is a bold reddish-brown color and comes in several forms: powder, chips, and sticks. The rigid bark is very hard to grind, so use powder for general baking, chips for grinding, and chips or sticks for infusions.

True cinnamon is a bit more rare of a find and is milder than its cassia cousins. Just because it is called true cinnamon does not mean it has better flavor or should be substituted for cassia cinnamon. This softer variety comes from Sri Lanka and is also known as Ceylon cinnamon. It is sold mainly in whole form and should not be purchased preground, as the delicate flavors are quickly lost. The more elusive essence of true cinnamon can be featured in all manner of dishes from appetizers to dessert—but be sure not to overwhelm it with other flavors. It is an exotic treat.

In the recipes in this book, we refer to cassia cinnamon simply as cinnamon, because that is what we use most commonly and the name by which it is typically sold. We will refer to true cinnamon as such. Look for it in our recipe for ras el hanout.

Using cinnamon for more than just baking will transform meat rubs, soups, and stews into entirely new creations. Cinnamon is an upfront player in blends like garam masala, besar, and baharat and plays more of a supporting role in curries, berbere, and harissa.

CLOVES

Cloves are one of the spice gems of the Moluccas in Indonesia. These little tree buds are very potent, and only a small bit is required to get a lot of flavor. Used sparingly as an accent ingredient, the warm tingle of cloves adds an invigorating pop to any dish. Use whole cloves for braising and infusions, and powdered cloves for baking.

CORIANDER SEED

This seed spice has been cultivated since ancient times and comes from the same plant that gives us cilantro leaves. The mellow flavor is smooth and savory, with creamy citrus top notes. Coriander is best purchased whole and is easy to grind. It can be toasted to enhance the flavor. Coriander is an integral part of the flavor base in curries, masalas, and mixes from throughout the Middle East, but it also performs well solo. Try it in granola and cereal mixes, or as part of a seasoning crust on fish.

CUMIN SEED

The humble cumin seed sprouts off the end of a weedy grass and is nearly as universal a seasoning as black pepper. Pungent and earthy, the savory base of cumin is surrounded by the lightest hints of citrus and pine, giving it a well-rounded and pleasing flavor. This seed spice has been cultivated since ancient times and is best kept whole to preserve its flavor and then ground before use. Intricate flavors develop nicely as cumin is cooked.

DILL WEED

Dill is another classic flavor that is familiar to many. Used fresh or dried, the lacy leaves of dill are delicate in texture and well-rounded in flavor. The combination of sour and sweet in this herbaceous plant is a unique and welcome addition sprinkled alone on seafood with just a squeeze of lemon or to enhance robust herbal blends like Israeli za'atar.

FENNEL SEED

"Vibrant green" describes both the color and the taste of fennel seeds. Their unique licorice-centric flavor will add distinctive sweetness when used as a single ingredient or as part of a blend. You will find them more dominant in blends like Chinese five-spice, while offering a hint of sweetness for contrast in blends like Kashmiri curry and besar.

FENUGREEK SEED

These hard square seeds may require an extra pulse in the grinder, but it's worth the effort. You'll often find them in curries and they make a notable contribution to berbere. Fenugreek conveys a mild, nutty, maple-like flavor that provides an interesting background note. They can be bitter if too many are added, so always use small amounts. Toasting can also mellow the bitterness.

GARLIC

Garlic is an essential ingredient in many dishes, and we are all familiar with its flavor and staying power. Fresh garlic is the ideal choice for pastes and marinades. We recommend using chopped or granulated garlic instead of garlic powder because it disperses more evenly and has better flavor.

GINGER

Ginger is a tropical rhizome that can be used fresh or dried, with different results. Both forms of ginger offer snappy heat, but the fresh grated root has a floral hint not found in the dried. If you are looking for concentrated heat, use the dried form. Fresh ginger can be easily grated or sliced and pounded into paste in a mortar and pestle. The fibers within the dried ginger rhizome make it challenging to grind, so preground ginger is the best choice for the dried form.

GRAINS OF PARADISE

Who can resist a name like that? This spice has been traded since medieval times, but became scarce when the easily cultivated black peppercorn dominated the spice market. The mythical flavor of grains of paradise is like a cross between pepper and cardamom, though it is botanically related to neither. Native to Africa, and a member of the ginger family, this exotic gem is shaped like a tiny popcorn kernel, and a good sign of freshness is when the point on the seed is intact. We use it in our ras el hanout—the showcase for our finest exotic spices—but if you don't have any on hand, substitute black peppercorns.

LAVENDER FLOWERS

Lavender flowers are most commonly used in French Provençal cuisine and have a distinctive bouquet that enhances herbal blends and delicate desserts.

LONG PEPPER

Long pepper is a rare and wonderful spice. Over the years, it has remained difficult to track down but is always worth the hunt. A botanical cousin to back pepper, the long pepper boasts a more complex flavor with hints of ginger and floral notes. The long fruit buds can be used whole for infusions or cracked for spice blends.

MARJORAM

Marjoram has wonderfully delicate flavors in both the fresh and dried forms. It is less sharp than its cousin oregano and has just the right balance of herbaceous undertones. It is featured in our dukkah blend, and we always keep some on hand. When using marjoram, always add a pinch in the final stage of cooking to capture the most elusive flavors.

MUSTARD SEED, BROWN OR BLACK

Mustard seeds add zesty flavor to sauces, dressings, and spice blends. When toasting the seeds, keep an eye out for when they begin to pop out of the pan as this signals they should be removed from the heat. The brown and black varieties can be used interchangeably and are hotter than their yellow cousins. Try leaving the seeds whole for spice rubs to experience their unusual texture and flavor. While commonly found in South Indian curries, mustard seeds are featured in our ras el hanout.

NIGELLA SEED

Also called kalonji, these quirky seeds offer a playful topping alternative to sesame seeds and are often sprinkled on naan flatbreads, vegetable dishes, and curries. A light toasting releases mild flavor and crunch. Nigella seeds are a welcome addition to salads and soups, and the black color and unusual shape makes for a fun garnish.

NUTMEG

Never buy preground nutmeg—instead buy the whole egg-shaped seeds. Preground nutmeg is flavorless compared to freshly grated because its flavors are so volatile. A Microplane grater, which can also be used for zesting citrus fruits, works beautifully for grating whole nutmeg and is easy to use. You will taste an incredible difference in all your culinary creations with the addition of fresh nutmeg. Nutmeg is a signature spice in many desserts and an essential accent in cream sauces. It is featured in both Kashmiri garam masala and baharat.

OREGANO

The bold flavors of oregano are present in both the fresh and dried forms of the herb, and there are many regional varieties to explore—Greek, Turkish, and Mexican to name a few. Our go-to is Turkish variety for its balanced flavor profile. It provides a vibrant herbal note in our Israeli za'atar.

PEPPERCORNS, BLACK

Black pepper is known as the king of spices along the Malabar Coast of India, its native home. This pure spice once traded for a price above gold and remains the most widely used spice in the world. It is included in virtually every blend on our list because it has such a universally appealing flavor. Dried black peppercorns should appear dark black and bold, not dull or faded. It should present a familiar heat on the tongue followed by a crisp, ethereal high note to finish.

PEPPERCORNS, SZECHUAN

Tingle is the word that best describes the remarkable sensation of Szechuan peppercorns on the tongue. This is complemented by a peppery heat on the palate (though Szechuan peppercorns are not botanically related to black pepper) with some floral characteristics on the high end of the flavor profile. A signature ingredient in Chinese five-spice, this unique spice can also be infused with dramatic effect into sweets, sauces, and cocktails.

ROSE PETALS

A bouquet of roses is unmistakable and is the essence of floral flavor. It is a signature flavor in Moroccan and Middle Eastern dishes. We've added rose petals to our ras el hanout for that extra special note. Be sure to separate the petals from the hips if you purchase roses, as the hips can be bitter. Rose petals make a lovely infusion in simple syrup.

SAFFRON

Saffron threads are the dried stigmas of the saffron crocus, and they are the most expensive spice in the world. Each small purple crocus yields only three brilliant red stigmas that must be carefully handpicked from the center of the flower, and a staggering number are required to make up even one ounce. As such, saffron is sold in smaller gram quantities. Intact bright-red threads with a bit of elasticity are sure signs of freshness.

Fortunately, just a few threads of saffron are enough to flavor a dish. We use it most often as a pure spice so that its powerful, elegant flavor may be fully appreciated. Saffron threads can be infused in a small amount of liquid, typically water or white wine, before use. This releases the saffron flavor and yellow color into the liquid, which brightens and enhances your dish.

STAR ANISE

The familiar flavor of star anise comes from the organic compound anethole, also found in anise seed, licorice, and fennel. Star anise has floral notes as well, which give it a sweet characteristic. A key ingredient in Chinese five-spice, star anise also has a range of uses all its own. It is easy to infuse into syrups and sauces and, because the whole spice is large and rather hard, is best used in this way. However, if you are going to grind it, crack it into smaller pieces in a mortar and pestle beforehand.

SUMAC

If you are looking for tart flavor, look no further. These Middle Eastern berries are found only in ground form, which distributes well into za'atar mixes and makes a beautiful garnish on dips and spreads. Good quality sumac should be a vibrant cabernet color and a bit sticky.

THYME

Thyme has a deep savory flavor that is present in both the fresh and dried herb. It is a key component in Israeli za'atar but can also be used on its own to add an aromatic, savory dimension to meat rubs, soups, and stews.

TURMERIC

Turmeric is a rhizome, like ginger, and is dried and ground into a resinous powder. Its deep golden-yellow color has become synonymous with the name and it is what gives yellow curries their color. The rich, earthy flavors that emerge from turmeric impart solid base and accent flavors to many blends.

VANILLA BEANS

These elegant orchid pods provide incredible flavor to desserts. While they are more costly and require a bit more effort to use than vanilla extract, the beans offer versatility and extra-special flavors. For example, you can scrape out the seeds to make an infusion, and then add the scraped pods to a jar of fine sugar to make vanilla sugar. Vanilla beans are cultivated in the most exotic locales, from Tahiti to Madagascar, and all are delicious. Oily and flexible pods are the signs of freshness you should look for.

SALT SELECTIONS

❧

While salt is technically not a spice, it is an essential ingredient—and lucky for us, the use of sea salts from around the globe has become all the rage.

When asked frankly—is there any difference? Isn't salt just salt? The answer is both yes and no. Refined table salt is sodium chloride, NaCl, pure and simple, with the possible addition of iodine, which has no impact on the taste. Kosher salt is also pure NaCl but without the iodine, and it is also free of aluminum products and anti-caking agents. Kosher salt is the best go-to choice for cooking, brining, and baking. It is free of additives and disperses well into any dish.

When it comes to sea salts, flavors begin to diversify. The mineral content of sea salts varies depending on where the salt was harvested. Sea salts are best appreciated when used at the end of the cooking process, for finishing dishes or even at the table.

The other sensory element offered by sea salts is texture. Some are specially harvested to produce delicate flakes, while others are coarse and chunky. Which ones to have on hand is a matter of personal taste, but from the dizzying array, these are our favorites.

....

FLAKE SALTS are best used for finishing because of their delicate texture. The larger flakes dissolve more slowly, adding a bit of salty crunch to cap off everything from roasted meats to heirloom tomatoes. Try a sprinkle on savory baked goods during the second half of the baking time for a spectacular topper. Best choices? **MURRAY RIVER**, **MALDON**, and **FLEUR DE SEL**.

COARSE SALTS can come in either wet or dry form and need to be ground a bit for most uses. We like to use them in rubs and crusts, as well as for finishing. Dry sea salts can go into a salt grinder, but wet ones are best ground in a mortar and pestle so as not to rust or clog the grinding mechanism. **HIMALAYAN SALT** is dry and comes in a range of sizes. It has a light apricot color and a robust mineral flavor. French grey sea salt, or **SEL DE MER**, has long been prized for its taste of the sea; it graced many a spice merchant's shelf long before the more recent salt craze. It remains a favorite for flavor and texture.

There is an abundance of flavored salts and seasoning salts out there—too many good ones to list. The only flavored salt that made the cut to "essential" status on our list is **ALDERWOOD SMOKED SALT**. This gem of the Northwest has an intense, true smoky flavor, and a little pinch can add incredibly robust flavor to any dish.

Spice Blends

Great spice blends are made when individual ingredients merge to create entirely new flavors. Whether it is a simple combination like Chinese five-spice or an intricate tapestry of flavor like ras el hanout, a taste of these blends will widen your eyes and enliven your palate. All of the blends presented here can vault your everyday cooking to that level.

Spices can be combined in an infinite number of ways, and the flavor possibilities that result are endless. To narrow the scope within the covers of a book, we have selected thirteen signature spice blends from the archives at World Spice Merchants. It is a well-rounded array of notable mixes from global cuisine, offering a range of flavor profiles to play with. All are time-tested blends—just like something out of your grandmother's recipe box—and they can be used just as easily.

We've included recipes for the spice blends so you can make them at home, but pre-blended versions are also available fresh and ready to go from World Spice Merchants or your favorite local vendor. If you choose to make them yourself, we recommend doing so ahead of time and keeping your favorites on hand. This is a real time saver in the kitchen. Having the blends at your fingertips ensures that you can add volumes of flavor in the blink of an eye. In the process, you'll be tempted to experiment . . . and we hope you do! Just like recipes for any favorite dish, these recipes can be adjusted to suit your taste.

We present a variety of ways to use each spice blend throughout the book. From sweet to savory and appetizers to desserts, a single blend can be used in many different dishes. No one wants to make or buy a spice blend to cook only one thing and have the remainder waste away on the shelf. That's why we decided to show the wide variety of meals you can cook with just a handful of spices and blends.

cinnamon

nutmeg

coriander

cumin

black pepper

allspice

Hungarian paprika

cardamom

cloves

BAHARAT

BAHARAT

The name *baharat* translates simply to mean "spices," and it is an all-purpose seasoning blend for Middle Eastern cuisine. But don't let the unassuming name and adaptable status fool you, because this blend has a lot to offer. Its contents vary regionally but are typically warm and sweet, calling to mind comfort foods cooking low and slow.

Our version starts with a base of cumin, coriander, and black pepper. These are combined with aromatic allspice, cinnamon, cardamom, nutmeg, and cloves for a well-rounded mixture of savory and sweet that develops nicely with longer cooking times.

Baharat brings out the best in any meat dish—especially lamb or beef. Try a teaspoon in your next burger or meatball dish. Better yet, add a pinch of salt and sugar and rub it on a rib-eye (see Seared Rib-Eye Steak with Baharat, page 151)! This spice blend can also be mixed with fresh herbs to make a paste, or used for flavoring condiments like our Turkish Sweet Onion Jam with Baharat (page 209).

MAKES ⅓ CUP

½ teaspoon whole cloves	1 teaspoon freshly grated nutmeg
1 tablespoon allspice berries	
1 tablespoon cumin seed	1 teaspoon ground cinnamon
1 tablespoon black peppercorns	1 teaspoon Hungarian paprika
2 teaspoons coriander seed	½ teaspoon cardamom seed

◆ In a mortar and pestle, crack the cloves into small pieces—this will allow them to disperse more evenly into the mix. Combine all the ingredients in a small bowl and mix well. Store in an airtight container and grind just before use. For additional depth of flavor, lightly toast and then cool the allspice, cumin, peppercorns, and coriander before combining with the other ingredients.

fenugreek

cloves

cardamom

nutmeg

ginger

Hungarian paprika

allspice

ajwain

cinnamon

garlic

turmeric

black pepper

coriander

African cayenne

BERBERE

Yes, the name is a bit of a tongue twister—pronounced bur-bur-uh—but this Ethiopian blend explodes with complex flavor. Berbere does have some heat, but don't turn away if you're not a fan of the flame. This blend offers spiciness and flavor in balanced measure, so whether you use it lightly or liberally, the array of complementary spices rounds out any dish.

In addition to a dose of heat from chile, ginger, and black peppercorns, berbere contains coriander, fenugreek, ajwain, turmeric, paprika, and garlic, with aromatic notes from allspice, cardamom, cinnamon, nutmeg, and cloves.

Traditionally used to season slow-cooked stews called *wats*, berbere enhances soups and stews of all varieties, and has a palatable flavor synergy with tomatoes. This makes berbere an ideal choice for condiments like Berbere Ketchup (page 207) and dishes with tomato-based sauces like Brisket with Berbere and Whiskey Barbecue Sauce (page 165). It also makes a great substitute for chile powder, harissa, or curry.

MAKES ½ CUP

1 teaspoon whole cloves	2 teaspoons Hungarian paprika
1 tablespoon coriander seed	2 teaspoons pequin chiles or
2 teaspoons fenugreek seed	African cayenne
2 teaspoons black	2 teaspoons garlic granules
peppercorns	1½ teaspoons ground ginger
1 teaspoon ajwain seed	½ teaspoon ground cinnamon
1 teaspoon allspice berries	1 teaspoon ground turmeric
1 teaspoon cardamom seed	1 teaspoon freshly grated nutmeg

- In a mortar and pestle, crack the cloves into small pieces—this will allow them to disperse more evenly into the mix. In a heavy dry pan over medium heat, toast the cloves, coriander, fenugreek, peppercorns, ajwain, and allspice until they are fragrant. Remove from the pan before they begin to smoke and allow to cool. Mix in the remaining ingredients. Store in an airtight container and grind just before use.

BESAR

Besar, also known as bzar or Emirati spice, is an intriguing and simple mixture that plays on several themes—it has a savory base of cumin and coriander, alongside warming, aromatic top notes of cinnamon and sweetness from fennel. Classic elements of South Indian curries are integrated into the besar with a hint of turmeric and chile. The whole mix is pungently toasted for maximum flavor like the richest garam masala. As a result, you end up with something entirely new. We love besar in practically everything, including our Besar Shrimp and Pineapple Skewers (page 67).

MAKES ½ CUP

2 tablespoons cinnamon chips	2 teaspoons coriander seed
1 tablespoon cumin seed	2 teaspoons black peppercorns
1 tablespoon fennel seed	½ teaspoon guajillo chile flakes
	2 teaspoons ground turmeric

◆ Mix together all the ingredients except the turmeric; toast them in a dry pan over medium heat, shaking the pan occasionally, until fragrant. Add the toasted spices to the turmeric while they are still warm and mix well. Allow the mixture to cool, and store in an airtight container. Grind just before use.

A WORD ABOUT CHILES AND CHILI POWDER

The term *chili powder* may cause confusion because it can have two different meanings. Americans most often think of chili powder as the thing you put in that distinctly American "bowl of red"—chili. In other parts of the world, the term often refers to pure ground chiles, either generally or specifically by name, like cayenne. Nowadays we often have the choice of chili powder made with all different types of the fiery fruit: chipotle (smoky), habañero (hot), ancho and guajillo (mild)—and they are all fabulous. So when a recipe calls for chili powder, check to see what makes sense; the origin of the recipe is usually the biggest clue. A Thai curry will rarely call for the blended version, whereas fajitas or tacos are typically looking for a mix.

black pepper

cinnamon

fennel

turmeric

chile flakes

coriander

cumin

BESAR

fennel

Szechuan pepper

star anise

cinnamon

cloves

CHINESE
FIVE-SPICE

CHINESE FIVE-SPICE

In Chinese culture, harmonious balance of the five elements—wood, fire, earth, metal, and water—is sought to foster radiant health and well-being. This philosophy is practiced in daily life through everything from feng shui to food. Chinese five-spice is a testament to their success, as it is truly a harmonious balance of flavors. Star anise, Szechuan peppercorns, fennel, cinnamon, and cloves are the only ingredients, yet the balanced synergy of this pungent mix offers a bouquet of flavors.

Traditionally used on fatty meats like duck and pork, Chinese five-spice can also be used to flavor desserts like Chinese Five-Spice Shortbread Cookies (page 194) or side dishes. It can be ground for use in cooking or as a rub, or used whole for aromatic infusions. This elemental blend is also a perfect base for additional seasonings—you can add more heat or more savory spices to take it in a whole new direction.

MAKES ABOUT ¼ CUP

1 tablespoon star anise
1½ teaspoons whole cloves
1 tablespoon fennel seed

1 tablespoon cinnamon chips or powder
1½ teaspoons Szechuan peppercorns

- In a mortar and pestle, crack the star anise and cloves into smaller pieces—this will allow them to disperse more evenly into the mix. Combine all the ingredients and store in an airtight container. Grind just before use.

CURRIES

Little-known fact: Most Indian kitchens don't have curry powder in the spice cabinet. The common Western misconception about curry is that it is a single spice—and nothing could be further from the truth. Curry (*kari* in Tamil) means "sauce," and this single item purchased in the states is actually a mixture of six to twelve ingredients, typically made in a South Indian style. In truth, curry has more regional variations than any other spice blend (as well as an unlimited range of flavor). In the kitchens of the subcontinent, cooks pinch and sprinkle from a palette of spices called a *masala dabba* and expertly vary the proportions according to the dish being prepared and its cooking time.

cardamom

chile flakes

fennel

coriander

cinnamon

turmeric

cloves

KASHMIRI CURRY

cumin

Perhaps one reason there are so many variations of curry is that there are so many things you can do with it. For any combination of meat and vegetables, there is a curry to complement it. From there, these diverse blends can be added to any course on the table, from appetizers to desserts—Kashmiri Curry Bread Pudding with Spiced Nuts (page 193), anyone?

The following spice-blend recipes are "yellow" curries in that they contain turmeric for its distinct flavor and hue, alongside the staples of cumin and coriander—but from there the flavors diverge.

Kashmiri Curry

At India's northern tip lies the cold and rugged Kashmir region. The curries here add warm spicing with extra cinnamon, cardamom, and cloves. We've added chile flakes as well and toned down the turmeric to let more of the aromatics shine through.

MAKES ⅓ CUP

½ teaspoon whole cloves
1 tablespoon cumin seed
1 tablespoon coriander seed
1 tablespoon fennel seed
1 tablespoon guajillo chile
   flakes

2 teaspoons cardamom
   seed
1½ teaspoons ground cinnamon
1 teaspoon ground turmeric

- In a mortar and pestle, crack the cloves into small pieces—this will allow them to disperse more evenly into the mix. Combine all the ingredients and store in an airtight container. Grind just before use.

cumin

cloves

coriander

black pepper

POUDRE DE COLOMBO

turmeric

fenugreek

rice

brown mustard seed

garlic

Hungarian paprika

black pepper

nutmeg

chile flakes

cardamom

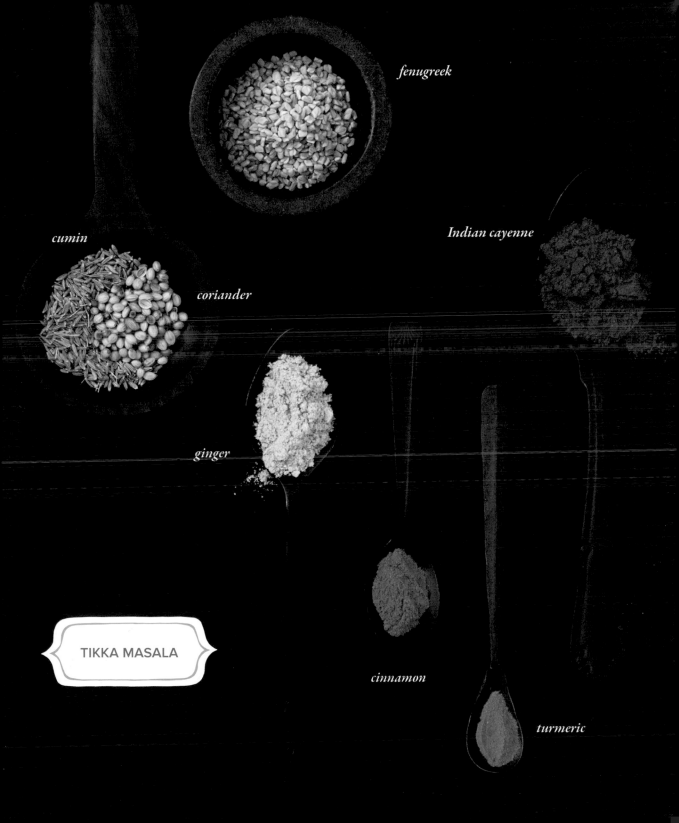

fenugreek

cumin

Indian cayenne

coriander

ginger

TIKKA MASALA

cinnamon

turmeric

Poudre de Colombo

This blend from the French West Indies is a lightly toasted mix made with black mustard seeds and fenugreek. Rice is included as a thickening agent for the soups and stews traditionally made with it.

MAKES ⅓ CUP

¼ teaspoon whole cloves

1 tablespoon cumin seed

2 teaspoons coriander seed

1½ teaspoons black peppercorns

1½ teaspoons fenugreek seed

1 teaspoon black mustard seed

1 tablespoon ground turmeric

1 tablespoon uncooked rice

◆ In a mortar and pestle, crack the cloves into small pieces—this will allow them to disperse more evenly into the mix. Toast the cloves, cumin, coriander, peppercorns, fenugreek, and mustard seed in a dry pan over medium heat. Shake the pan and continue toasting until the spices are browned and fragrant. Transfer to a medium bowl and sprinkle the turmeric over the warm spices. Toast the rice in the same pan and add it to the mix while hot. The heat from the spices and rice lightly toasts the turmeric for an evenly roasted mix. Store in an airtight container.

A WORD ABOUT REGIONAL VARIATIONS

We have a book on the shelf at World Spice Merchants called *660 Curries*. It's incredible. While you may not need quite that many at your fingertips at any given time, it illustrates the point that spice blend variations can be endless, especially when combined with the different ways to use them. When you look up a recipe for berbere or baharat, you'll find definitive themes because each blend has a distinct flavor profile—but quite a few ingredients may vary. Experimenting with variations is a great way to find new flavors. They say variety is the spice of life, and in this case it is quite literally true.

Tikka Masala

Tikka masala refers to both a popular dish and the spice blend used to season it. Surprisingly, neither is originally from India. Once the Brits got a taste of the Malabar Coast, cooks back home came up with tikka masala to satisfy their appetites and were wildly successful. Now you can find tikka masala in England as commonly as fish and chips. Ginger and paprika are included in our mix, along with a host of aromatics and chile flakes to tickle the taste buds.

MAKES ½ CUP

1 tablespoon plus 1 teaspoon ginger powder

1 tablespoon plus 1 teaspoon garlic granules

1 tablespoon cumin seed

1 tablespoon Hungarian paprika

2 teaspoons fenugreek seed

1½ teaspoons guajillo chile flakes

1½ teaspoons cardamom seed

1½ teaspoons freshly grated nutmeg

1 teaspoon coriander seed

1 teaspoon black peppercorns

½ teaspoon ground turmeric

½ teaspoon Indian cayenne

½ teaspoon ground cinnamon

◆ In a small bowl, combine all the ingredients and mix well. Store in an airtight container and grind just before use.

thyme

cumin

marjoram

coriander

hazelnuts

white sesame

black pepper

flake salt

DUKKAH

DUKKAH

This Egyptian spice blend combines toasted spices, hazelnuts, and dried herbs with salt and sesame seeds for a deeply satisfying flavor and texture. Traditionally, bread is dipped first in olive oil and then in dukkah for a simple bite packed with flavor. Dukkah reveals the best from cumin, coriander, thyme, and marjoram. Try using dukkah for all manner of crusts and rubs, or anywhere a salty and savory crunch would be nice. A little dukkah sprinkled on salads or as a crust for goat cheese or tuna is a simple way to enhance their inherent flavors.

MAKES ½ CUP

¼ cup chopped hazelnuts

2 tablespoons white sesame seeds

2 tablespoons cumin seed

1½ tablespoons coriander seed

½ teaspoon black peppercorns

2 teaspoons dried marjoram

1 teaspoon dried thyme leaves

1 to 2 teaspoons flake or kosher salt

- In a dry pan over medium heat, toast the hazelnuts and sesame seeds until golden; transfer to a medium bowl and set aside to cool. In the same pan, toast the cumin, coriander, and peppercorns until fragrant. Transfer to a small bowl and allow to cool. Pulse the cumin mixture in an electric mill to a medium-fine grind, then combine them with the hazelnuts. Mix in the marjoram, thyme, and salt. Store in an airtight container. Use as is for sprinkling on salads, or grind to the desired consistency for crusts and rubs just before use.

chile flakes

smoked paprika

garlic

cinnamon

cumin

coriander

salt

Hungarian paprika

caraway

African càyenne

HARISSA

HARISSA

Once you introduce harissa into your spice cabinet, it will be stocked there forever. This extraordinary spice blend comes to us from North Africa and is similar to the "chili powder" used in American cuisine, but it has more complexity and depth of flavor. Harissa is a combination of paprika, dried chiles, and other spices, and ours is blended to impart mild heat and rich accents. Try this blend in all your favorite dishes calling for chili powder and you will be thrilled with the results—it is like having a whole new set of recipes.

We will show you how to turn harissa into a flavorful paste to use as a condiment, in sauces and glazes like our Oven-Roasted Chicken with Harissa-Honey Glaze (page 173). Harissa can be used as a seasoning on everything from the lightest white fish to the boldest beef brisket simply by varying the proportion according to the intensity of flavor desired. It's also a delicious surprise on spiced nuts, deviled eggs, or sprinkled on a casserole.

MAKES ½ CUP

1 tablespoon caraway seed	2 teaspoons smoked paprika
2 teaspoons coriander seed	1½ teaspoons Hungarian paprika
1 teaspoon cumin seed	1 teaspoon pequin chiles
2 tablespoons guajillo chile flakes	or African cayenne
2 teaspoons chopped fresh garlic	½ teaspoon ground cinnamon

♦ In a dry pan over medium heat, toast the caraway, coriander, and cumin until fragrant. Transfer to a small bowl and set aside to cool. Combine with the remaining ingredients and store in an airtight container. Grind just before use.

KASHMIRI GARAM MASALA

The name *garam masala* translates to mean "hot mixture," referring to the intensity of the warming spices that comprise it. There are actually no chiles in the mix—rather, it's a potent combination of aromatic spices including cinnamon, cardamom, peppercorns, and cloves. This classic blend has many regional variations and is included in all manner of traditional curries and pilafs. Our favorite is this Kashmiri blend, darkly roasted and intense. Try it in anything chocolate, like our Kashmiri Garam Masala–Infused Chocolate Truffles (page 186), and you'll be delighted with the results.

This toasted blend requires a careful hand with the pan to prevent burning. The spices are toasted sequentially in small batches to get the darkest roast on each without scorching them.

MAKES ½ CUP

1 teaspoon whole cloves	1 tablespoon plus 1 teaspoon coriander seed
2 tablespoons cardamom seed	1 tablespoon plus 1 teaspoon cinnamon chips
2 teaspoons cumin seed	1 tablespoon freshly grated nutmeg
2 teaspoons black peppercorns	

◆ In a mortar and pestle, crack the cloves into small pieces—this will allow them to disperse more evenly into the mix. In a dry pan, toast the cloves and cardamom until they just begin to smoke. If you see ashes begin to form on the cloves, remove from the heat immediately and transfer to a small bowl to cool—this is a sign that they are about to burn. In the same pan, toast the cumin and peppercorns until dark and smoking but not burned. Transfer to a small bowl and allow to cool. Finally, toast the coriander and cinnamon chips until dark and smoking. Allow to cool slightly and then add the nutmeg. Combine all the spices and mix well. Store in an airtight container and grind just before use.

cinnamon

cloves

KASHMIRI
GARAM MASALA

cardamom

black pepper

cumin

coriander

nutmeg

cardamom

cumin

long pepper

coriander

brown mustard seed

true cinnamon

ajwain

rose petals

nutmeg

black pepper

caraway

chamomile flowers

lavender

grains of paradise

fenugreek

cloves

RAS EL HANOUT

anise seed

Hungarian paprika

ginger

nigella

allspice

RAS EL HANOUT

We all love a good mystery, and it's doubly true in the case of a secret ingredient: plainly there for us to taste but elusively masked within the dish. From grandma's spaghetti sauce to the closely guarded formula for Coca-Cola, the notion of a secret blend of flavors has always captured the collective imagination. Grandma wasn't the first to have a secret recipe. Long before, spice merchants in North African bazaars had adopted the practice of showcasing their finest ingredients in a single exclusive blend, sold under the lofty title "head of the shop," or ras el hanout.

Our ras el hanout combines savory undertones with sweet top notes among a light swirl of floral ether and peaks of pepper. Really, it has it all . . . and a deft hand with this spice mix will always leave your guests wondering, "What *is that*?"

MAKES ¾ CUP

1 tablespoon dried rose petals	2 teaspoons grains of paradise
1 teaspoon cracked long pepper	1½ teaspoons ground turmeric
½ teaspoon whole cloves	1 teaspoon dried lavender flowers
½ stick true cinnamon	1 teaspoon dried chamomile flowers
1 tablespoon plus 1 teaspoon cumin seed	1 teaspoon nigella seed
1 tablespoon plus 1 teaspoon coriander seed	1 teaspoon brown mustard seed
1 tablespoon black peppercorns	1 teaspoon ground ginger
1 tablespoon allspice berries	1 teaspoon caraway seed
1 tablespoon freshly grated nutmeg	½ teaspoon fenugreek seed
1 tablespoon Hungarian paprika	½ teaspoon cardamom seed
	½ teaspoon ajwain seed
	½ teaspoon anise seed

♦ To prepare for mixing, check to see if your rose petals are still attached to the base of the buds. If they are, remove the hips and add only the rose petals to your blend. In a mortar and pestle, crack the long pepper and cloves into small pieces and transfer to a medium bowl. Crumble in the true cinnamon. Add the remaining ingredients and mix well. Store in an airtight container and grind just before use.

dill

ISRAELI ZA'ATAR

oregano

thyme

sumac

white sesame

sea salt

SYRIAN ZA'ATAR

sea salt

sumac

anise seed

coriander

white sesame

cumin

ZA'ATAR

Working around spices every day, we at World Spice Merchants don't always notice their astounding background aromas—but the magic moment when the bouquet of za'atar rises from the mixing bowls always captures our attention. Za'atar is a popular blend in Middle Eastern cuisine and there are many regional variations. It is often a strikingly simple combination that reveals more than the sum of its parts. The most widely used versions start with an herbal blend of thyme, oregano, and dill that contrasts with the tartness of sumac and savory peaks of salt. All of these flavors balance on a warm, earthy base of toasted sesame seeds. Za'atar blends from Syria contain more sumac, less herbs, and are more intensely tart.

Za'atar is a classic table condiment and commonly adorns flatbreads, either being mixed into the dough or sprinkled on top. It can be used in any meal of the day and is most successful when it can show off rather than remain subtle. While it can be cooked into a dish or used as a meat rub, shorter cooking times allow za'atar to take center stage, such as when it's sprinkled on warm meats just removed from the oven. Garnishing bean, grain, Greek, or potato salads with za'atar is another great use. It is also a fabulous seasoning for croutons and popcorn.

The truth? You'll find yourself eating this blend straight out of the jar.

Israeli Za'atar

MAKES ½ CUP

¼ cup white sesame seeds	1 teaspoon dried thyme leaves
1 tablespoon dried Turkish oregano	½ teaspoon kosher or sea salt
1 teaspoon dried dill	1 tablespoon sumac

- In a dry pan over medium heat, toast the sesame seeds until evenly browned, then transfer them to a small bowl. Allow to cool completely. In another small bowl, mix together 1½ tablespoons of the toasted seeds with the oregano, dill, thyme, and salt. Pulse the mixture in an electric mill until the sesame seeds have broken down and have blended with the herbs. Transfer the mixture back to the bowl and add the sumac, massaging out any lumps with your fingers. Add the remaining sesame seeds and stir well. Store in an airtight container and use as is.

Syrian Za'atar

MAKES ½ CUP

2 tablespoons coriander seed	2 teaspoons kosher or sea salt
1 teaspoon cumin seed	1½ tablespoons white sesame seeds
1 teaspoon anise seed	
2 tablespoons sumac	

◆ In a dry pan over medium heat, toast the coriander, cumin, and anise until lightly browned and fragrant. Transfer to a small bowl and allow to cool completely. Grind the toasted spices to a medium-fine consistency in an electric mill. Return to the bowl and add the sumac and salt, massaging out any lumps with your fingers. In the same pan, toast the sesame seeds. Transfer to another small bowl and allow to cool completely, then add to the spice mixture. Store in an airtight container and use as is.

PURE SPICE RECIPES

❦

Heirloom Tomato Gazpacho with Urfa Biber	79	Nectarine Upside-Down Cake with Cardamom Custard	181
Udon Noodle Bowl with Prawns in Star Anise Broth	91	Peach Cobbler with Nutmeg, Cardamom, and Cinnamon	197
Summer Tomato Salad with Arugula and Urfa Biber	103	Lavender Pavlovas with Blackberries and Cream	201
Crispy Jicama and Watermelon Salad with Sumac	114	Sunshine Vinaigrette with Sumac and Aleppo	204
Five-Seed Roasted Potatoes	118	Apricot and Coriander Salad Dressing	205
Halibut Poached in Olive Oil with Saffron	130	Wirtabel's Melon Chutney	208
Spicy Shrimp and Grits	147	Spiced Rhubarb-Orange Marmalade	214
Amanda's Cumin-Crusted Cornbread	179	Chile-Infused Oil	217
		Niter Kibbeh Spiced Butter	219

SPICE-BLEND RECIPES

❦

BAHARAT

Picadillo Peppers with Baharat	61	Braised Beef Short Ribs with Caramelized Onions and Baharat	161
Irresistible Spiced Nuts	71	Turkish Sweet Onion Jam with Baharat	209
Seared Rib-Eye Steak with Baharat	151		

BERBERE

Spicy Chili with Berbere	92	Brisket with Berbere and Whiskey Barbecue Sauce	165
Pan-Fried Sole with Berbere and Lemon Butter	135	Berbere Sloppy Joes	176

continued

Berbere Ketchup	207	Niter Kibbeh Spiced Butter	219

BESAR

Besar Shrimp and Pineapple Skewers	67	Maple-Glazed Pork Chops with Besar	153
Golden Butternut Squash Soup with Besar	85	Melt-in-Your-Mouth Pot Roast with Besar and Spaetzle	171
Sausage, White Bean, and Kale Soup with Besar	89	Gingerbread Cake with Besar and Caramel Pears	191

CHINESE FIVE-SPICE

Chinese Five-Spice Chicken Wings with Chili-Garlic Sauce	75	Chinese Five-Spice Shortbread Cookies	194
Pork Ribs with Chinese Five-Spice and Barbecue Sauce	155	Apple Galette with Chinese Five-Spice	198
Grilled Steak Salad with Chinese Five-Spice	166		

CURRIES

Creamy Cauliflower and Leek Soup with Tikka Masala	88	Dungeness Crab Melts with Kashmiri Curry	133
Parsnip and Potato Soup with Poudre de Colombo	93	Coconut-Steamed Mussels with Tikka Masala	137
Bubble and Squeak with Poudre de Colombo	105	Skillet Prawns with Poudre de Colombo	138
Quinoa with Grilled Vegetables and Kashmiri Dressing	112	Baked Chicken with Tikka Masala Sauce	169
Potato and Spinach Roll-Ups with Poudre de Colombo	119	Kashmiri Curry Bread Pudding with Spiced Nuts	193
		Basic Curry Paste	218

DUKKAH

Pogacha Flatbread with Sea Salt and Dukkah	59		

continued

Crostini with Dukkah-Encrusted Goat
Cheese and Roasted Tomatoes   69

Roasted Beet Salad with Watercress
and Dukkah Goat Cheese   99

Dukkah-Encrusted Seared Scallops   123

HARISSA

Fisherman's Stew with Harissa   95

Crisp Oven-Roasted Broccoli
with Lemon and Harissa   101

Steamed True Cod
with Harissa-Garlic Sauce   125

Oyster Po' Boys
with Harissa and Muffuletta   141

Shellfish Paella with Harissa
and Urfa Biber   145

Oven-Roasted Chicken
with Harissa-Honey Glaze   173

Classic Harissa Paste   213

KASHMIRI GARAM MASALA

Lollapalooza Lamb Sliders with
Berbere Ketchup   63

Pan-Roasted Halibut with
Kashmiri Garam Masala Glaze   143

Pumpkin Custard with Kashmiri
Garam Masala and Maple Cream   184

Kashmiri Garam Masala–Infused
Chocolate Truffles   186

Moist Carrot Cake with Kashmiri
Garam Masala   189

RAS EL HANOUT

Honey-Glazed Eggplant
with Ras el Hanout   109

Kale Tabbouleh with Pomegranate
Seeds and Ral el Hanout Dressing   117

Pork Tenderloin with Ras el Hanout and
Urfa Biber Sweet Potatoes   158

Ras el Hanout Spice Paste   211

Apple Butter with Ras el Hanout   212

ZA'ATAR

Za'atar Fries with Lemon-Pepper Aioli   73

Corn Chowder with
Chanterelles, Bacon, and Za'atar   81

Crimson Beet and Apple
Soup with Za'atar Cream   83

Vegetable Bread Salad with Za'atar   107

Grilled Salmon with Za'atar
and Sauce Gribiche   127

Crusted Rack of Lamb
with Syrian Za'atar   163

Small Bites

Pogacha Flatbread
with Sea Salt and Dukkah 59

Picadillo Peppers with Baharat 61

Lollapalooza Lamb Sliders
with Berbere Ketchup 63

Besar Shrimp and
Pineapple Skewers 67

Crostini with Dukkah-
Encrusted Goat Cheese
and Roasted Tomatoes 69

Irresistible Spiced Nuts 71

Za'atar Fries with
Lemon-Pepper Aioli 73

Chinese Five-Spice Chicken
Wings with Chili-Garlic Sauce 75

POGACHA FLATBREAD WITH SEA SALT & DUKKAH

———

Pogacha is fast and easy; it will become your go-to bread. This Serbian version of traditional flatbread is enhanced by the nuttiness of the dukkah, accented by its coriander and sesame seeds. Serve with olives, a soft cheese spread, and spiced nuts.

MAKES 5 TO 6 FLATBREADS

1 cup milk, warmed slightly, divided
2 teaspoons active dry yeast
1 teaspoon sugar

2¼ cups all-purpose flour, plus more for dusting
1 teaspoon kosher salt
3 tablespoons yogurt
2 tablespoons butter, melted

¼ cup extra-virgin olive oil, for brushing
¼ teaspoon sea salt for each flatbread
1½ teaspoons dukkah for each flatbread

- In a small bowl, stir together ½ cup of the warm milk (if the milk is too hot it will kill the yeast, so just heat slightly above room temperature), yeast, and sugar. Let stand for 5 minutes.

- In a large bowl, stir together the flour and kosher salt. Make a well in the center of the flour, and add the yogurt, melted butter, remaining ½ cup warm milk, and the yeast mixture. Using your hands or a spatula, take the flour from the outside and work it into the center, slowly folding the dough in on itself, always working in a circular motion.

- Once it has formed into a ball, turn it out onto a lightly floured surface. Start kneading by working the heel of your hand into the center of the dough, pushing outward. Fold the dough over itself and push outward again with the heel of your hand. Keep doing this for about 5 minutes, only adding more flour if the dough is really sticky. You want the dough to have a little tackiness to it. Knead until the dough is smooth.

continued

- Put the dough in a large, lightly oiled bowl, cover with a tea towel or plastic wrap, and allow to rise for at least 1 hour at room temperature, or until it has doubled in size.

- Position an oven rack in the top third of the oven. Lightly oil a pizza stone or the bottom of a cast-iron skillet and place it on the rack. Preheat the oven to 500 degrees F.

- Punch down the dough. Transfer it to a lightly floured surface. Cut into 5 pieces and roll each piece into an 8-by-5-inch oblong shape (the pieces don't have to be precisely the same shape or size). Using hot mitts, pull the oven rack out just a little bit. Carefully add 1 or 2 of the flatbreads to the pizza stone; bake until golden brown bubbles form, about 5 minutes. Using tongs, flip the breads over and cook for another 3 to 4 minutes. Remove the breads from the oven, brush with a couple teaspoons of olive oil, and sprinkle with the sea salt and dukkah. Repeat with the rest of the dough. Cut into wedges and serve with your favorite spreads and extra-virgin olive oil on the side.

> NOTE: You can also heat a skillet on the stovetop to cook the breads. Lightly oil the skillet and place over medium-high heat. Add one rolled-out dough, cover with a lid, and cook for 4 to 5 minutes. Using tongs, flip it over and cook for about 4 more minutes. Remove from the skillet and proceed with the recipe as written.

PICADILLO PEPPERS
WITH BAHARAT

———— ••• ————

Picadillo is a traditional dish in Spain and Latin America. We've created our own version using baharat, which adds notes of cumin, coriander, and allspice to the meat. These stuffed peppers make a colorful and delicious appetizer. Once you have the picadillo made, the assembly is so easy. The size of the peppers makes them easy for guests to pick up and eat. The filling is also perfect for mini pita pockets or tacos, with the addition of finely chopped romaine lettuce and your favorite cheese sprinkled on top!

MAKES 2 DOZEN SMALL PEPPER HALVES

FOR THE PICADILLO:

3 tablespoons golden raisins

2 tablespoons extra-virgin olive oil

½ yellow onion, finely chopped

1 tablespoon minced garlic

1 tablespoon ground baharat

1 pound ground beef or lamb

1 (28-ounce) can crushed tomatoes in puree

½ cup pimento-stuffed green olives, finely chopped

2 tablespoons tomato paste

1 tablespoon brown sugar

FOR THE PEPPERS:

¼ cup pine nuts

1 dozen mini bell peppers, halved, seeded, white membrane removed

2 tablespoons extra-virgin olive oil

Kosher salt and freshly ground black pepper

• To make the picadillo, first put the raisins in a bowl and cover with hot water. Let sit for 10 to 15 minutes, then drain and set the raisins aside.

• Heat the olive oil over medium-low heat in a large cast-iron skillet. Add the onion and cook for about 5 minutes. Add the garlic and baharat and cook for 3 minutes, stirring often. Add the ground beef, breaking it up into small pieces with a large wooden spoon, and cook for 5 minutes, or until golden, spooning out any excess liquid after the meat is partially cooked. Add the tomatoes with

continued

puree, green olives, tomato paste, brown sugar, and raisins; simmer over low heat for about 30 minutes, or until any liquid has been absorbed and the picadillo starts to thicken. Remove from the heat.

♦ Preheat the oven to 400 degrees F.

♦ Put the pine nuts into a frying pan set over medium-low heat. Give the pan a few shakes and cook until they are mostly golden. Transfer to a plate to cool.

♦ Arrange the peppers on a foil-lined baking sheet, cut side up, and drizzle with the olive oil. Season with salt and pepper. Fill each pepper half with 1 heaping tablespoon picadillo mixture, then sprinkle with a bit more salt and pepper and bake for 15 to 20 minutes, or until the peppers soften and the skins just start to wrinkle. Remove from the oven and top with a few pine nuts. Serve warm.

LOLLAPALOOZA LAMB SLIDERS WITH BERBERE KETCHUP

Everyone loves a good slider—and these are a great example of the perfect bite. A small soft bun surrounds moist lamb delicately seasoned with toasted spices. Then you get the unexpected flavor punch of berbere in the ketchup to top it off. Delicious! You can cook these sliders on the grill, but they brown up beautifully in a cast-iron pan. The dry, even heat creates a beautiful golden outside and perfectly cooked and moist inside.

MAKES 8 SLIDERS

FOR THE SPREAD:
½ cup mayonnaise
1 tablespoon
   Worcestershire
   sauce
1 tablespoon freshly
   squeezed lemon
   juice

FOR THE SLIDERS:
3 to 4 tablespoons
   extra-virgin olive oil,
   divided

1 red bell pepper,
   cored, seeded, and
   cut into ½-inch
   strips
1 sweet onion, sliced
   into ½-inch rings
2 pounds ground lamb
2 cloves garlic, minced
2 teaspoons ground
   Kashmiri garam
   masala
1 teaspoon kosher salt

1 teaspoon freshly
   ground pepper
8 mini brioche buns,
   brushed lightly with
   extra-virgin olive oil
   or butter
Berbere Ketchup
   (page 207)
½ cup pepperoncini
   rings, plus ½ cup
   whole pepperoncini,
   for serving

- To make the spread, in a small bowl, mix together the mayonnaise, Worcestershire sauce, and lemon juice until combined. Cover and place in the refrigerator.

- To make the lamb sliders, in a 10- to 12-inch skillet, heat 2 tablespoons of the olive oil over medium heat. Add the bell pepper and onion and cook, stirring, for about 15 minutes, or until they start to soften and the onions turn golden. Transfer to a plate and cover loosely with foil.

continued

- In a medium bowl, add the ground lamb and garlic. Sprinkle the garam masala, salt, and pepper all over the meat and mix with your hands. Do not overmix—just enough to combine the ingredients. Form the lamb into 4-by-1-inch patties.

- Preheat the broiler. Place the buns on a baking sheet and toast lightly in the oven, watching closely so they don't burn. Set aside.

- Heat the oven to 350 degrees F.

- Heat 1 tablespoon of the olive oil in a 10- to 12-inch cast-iron skillet over medium-high heat. Add the lamb patties, working in 2 batches (or use 2 skillets) if you can't fit all the patties in without crowding them. Cook for 5 minutes per side. Transfer all of the patties onto a baking sheet and bake for 5 minutes, or until a touch to the center of the meat slowly springs back. They should not be too firm or soft (there should be no lingering indentation after gently pressing down). Transfer to a plate, sprinkle with additional salt and pepper, and cover loosely with foil.

- To assemble the burgers, spread 1 tablespoon of the mayonnaise mixture on each side of the buns. Spread 2 teaspoons Berbere Ketchup on both sides. Place a patty on the bottom bun and top it with about 2 tablespoons of the onion mixture and 1 tablespoon pepperoncini rings. Serve immediately with whole pepperoncini on the side.

BESAR SHRIMP
& PINEAPPLE SKEWERS

The combination of exotic spices on seafood served with pineapple will transport you straight to the tropics. The bright layers of citrus and spice blend perfectly into the coconut oil and onto the shrimp. If you don't have time to skewer, just add the shrimp and pineapple to your indoor grill pan and serve on a platter with toothpicks. You can also turn this into a main dish by serving with steamed or grilled vegetables and rice.

MAKES 12 SKEWERS

FOR THE MARINADE:
¼ cup coconut or extra-virgin olive oil
¼ cup freshly squeezed lemon juice
2 cloves garlic, minced
2 tablespoons ground besar

1 teaspoon lemon zest
1 teaspoon Hungarian paprika
½ teaspoon kosher salt

FOR THE SHRIMP:
24 extra-large or large shrimp, peeled and deveined, tails intact

12 (6-inch) bamboo skewers
1 ripe pineapple
2 tablespoons extra-virgin olive oil, for brushing
2 teaspoons thyme, for garnish

- To make the marinade, melt the coconut oil in a small pan and allow it to cool to room temperature. In a large bowl, combine the lemon juice, garlic, besar, lemon zest, paprika, and salt, and whisk well. Slowly add the oil whisking to combine. Add the shrimp and gently toss to coat. Cover and place in the refrigerator for 30 minutes to 1 hour.

- Meanwhile, soak the skewers in water, placing a small plate directly on top of them to keep them completely submerged. Soak for about 20 minutes.

continued

- Cut the top and bottom off the pineapple and remove the rind. Halve the pineapple; cut one half into small wedges or 3- to 4-inch cubes. Cut the other half into larger wedges or half rings for serving.

- Remove the skewers from the water. Thread a shrimp onto a skewer through the tail, then through the top. Push the shrimp down toward the bottom, leaving enough room to grasp the skewer. Add a pineapple cube and then another shrimp. Place the skewer on a baking sheet. Repeat with the rest of the shrimp and pineapple. Add any extra pineapple to the skewers. Brush the pineapple cubes with a little olive oil.

- Heat an outdoor grill or indoor grill pan to medium-high heat. Cook the skewers for 3 to 4 minutes per side. Brush them with any extra marinade. Transfer to a platter, sprinkle with thyme, and serve with the pineapple wedges.

> NOTE: Either tikka masala or Kashmiri curry can be substituted for the besar to make this recipe with different flavors, or try orange juice and zest in place of the lemon. Add ½ teaspoon turmeric to the marinade if you want the prawns to have a brighter yellow color.

CROSTINI WITH DUKKAH-ENCRUSTED GOAT CHEESE & ROASTED TOMATOES

———— ◆ ————

These festive and flavorful small bites feature dukkah as a savory complement to the goat cheese, and mild chiles and fresh herbs to enhance the tomatoes. Bring them both together on a crispy crostini for a delicious treat. For additional flavor and crunch, you can serve with Irresistible Spiced Nuts (page 71).

MAKES 8 TO 10 SERVINGS

FOR THE TOMATOES:
1 clove garlic, minced
2 tablespoons extra-virgin olive oil
1 pint cherry tomatoes, stems removed
Leaves from 5 sprigs fresh thyme
Needles from 1 sprig fresh rosemary, roughly chopped
½ teaspoon fleur de sel or kosher salt
⅛ teaspoon urfa biber
Freshly ground black pepper

FOR THE CROSTINI:
½ cup extra-virgin olive oil
2 cloves garlic, minced
¼ teaspoon kosher salt

1 baguette or ciabatta bread, cut into 1-inch slices

FOR THE CHEESE:
¼ cup dukkah
¼ teaspoon sea salt
1 (8-ounce) log soft chèvre
1 cup pitted nicoise or kalamata olives

◆ Preheat the oven to 325 degrees F.

◆ To prepare the tomatoes, combine the garlic and olive oil in a small bowl and let it sit for about 10 minutes. Put the tomatoes in a medium bowl and drizzle with the infused oil. Sprinkle with the thyme, rosemary, fleur de sel, urfa biber, and pepper. Toss to coat. Spread the tomatoes on a foil-lined baking sheet and bake for 25 to 30 minutes, or until they start to split and the skins become golden in spots and slightly wrinkled.

continued

- To prepare the crostini, in a small bowl, combine the olive oil, garlic, and kosher salt. Using a pastry brush, lightly brush both sides of the bread slices with the oil. Heat a lightly greased grill pan or a barbecue over medium heat. Arrange a few bread slices in the pan and press down with a metal spatula to get grill marks. Cook for 2 to 3 minutes per side, or until lightly golden brown. Place the crostini on a cooling rack so they crisp up and don't get soft.

- To prepare the cheese, in a small bowl, mix the dukkah and sea salt. Spread the mixture on a large plate or baking sheet and roll the chèvre in it, pressing down to push the spices into the cheese without crumbling the log.

- To serve, place the crostini on a platter. Spread each crostini with 1 tablespoon chèvre and top with 2 to 3 roasted tomatoes and 2 olives.

IRRESISTIBLE SPICED NUTS

Spiced nuts are great just on their own or on salads. They can be crushed and used to encrust fish or lamb chops. They also make a welcome topping on many desserts. You can substitute different spice blends in this recipe to suit your tastes and intended use. Try curry on cashews for a salad or Kashmiri garam masala on pecans to adorn desserts.

MAKES 4 CUPS

⅓ cup granulated sugar

⅓ cup brown sugar

1 tablespoon ground baharat

1½ teaspoons kosher salt

1 egg white

4 cups raw mixed nuts (about 1 pound)

- Preheat oven to 250 degrees F.

- In a medium bowl, combine the sugars, baharat, and salt and mix well. In another medium bowl, whisk the egg white until airy, frothy, and light peaks form. Fold the nuts into the egg white until they are completely coated. Add the spice blend and stir with a spatula until the nuts are evenly coated.

- Spread the nuts in a single layer on a lightly oiled foil-lined baking sheet, using a spatula to scrape out any extra spices left in the bowl. Bake for 45 to 50 minutes, stirring several times during baking to coat the nuts well. Remove from the oven and let cool completely. If not using immediately, transfer to an airtight container; the nuts will keep for up to 2 weeks.

TIP: If you are using walnuts, try blanching them first for 2 to 3 minutes to remove the bitter skin, then roast in the oven for 10 minutes at 250 degrees F to dry them out. If using hazelnuts, you will want to remove the outer skins by roasting at 350 degrees F for 15 minutes, or until the skins start to crack, darken, and pull away from the nuts. Once cool enough to handle, put ½ cup hazelnuts in a kitchen towel and rub to remove the skins. Proceed with the recipe as written.

ZA'ATAR FRIES
WITH LEMON-PEPPER AIOLI

Deep fat frying can take time, and it's not something you do often. But when you do, you want it to count. These fries are worth the effort and will get consumed quickly! Keep kids away from the stove when frying and heat the oil on the back burner just to be safe. The za'atar takes french fries to a whole new level. You can also use dukkah or any type of curry. Try using sweet potatoes or eggplant with harissa or baharat!

MAKES 6 SERVINGS

FOR THE AIOLI:
¼ cup extra-virgin olive oil
¼ cup canola oil
1 large egg (or substitute ¼ cup pasteurized liquid eggs)
1 clove garlic, minced

2 tablespoons freshly squeezed lemon juice
¼ teaspoon kosher salt
¼ teaspoon freshly ground pepper

FOR THE FRIES:
4 pounds large russet potatoes, scrubbed

About 4 cups safflower, canola, or peanut oil, for frying
2 tablespoons Israeli or Syrian za'atar
Sea salt

+ To make the aioli, combine the oils in a measuring cup with a spout. Put the egg, garlic, and lemon juice in a blender and blend for just a few seconds. With the blender running and the lid on (center piece removed), slowly add the oil, about 1 tablespoon at a time. After adding half of the oil this way, add the rest in a slow, steady stream. If the aioli gets too thick, add 1 to 2 teaspoons of water or lemon juice. Transfer to a bowl and stir in the salt and pepper.

+ To make the fries, if you don't have a french-fry cutter, simply cut a slice off each long side of a potato, just enough so it lays flat. Cut the potatoes lengthwise into ½-inch slices. Then, stacking 4 slices at a time, cut crosswise into ½-inch sticks. Place in a large pot of cold water. Allow the potatoes to sit in the water for at least 1 to 2 hours.

continued

- Drain the potatoes and place them on paper towel–lined baking sheets. Blot the potatoes with additional paper towels to dry them. Place another paper towel–lined baking sheet next to the fryer.

- Add enough oil to come one-third of the way up the sides of a deep, heavy pot. Attach a deep-fry thermometer to the pot and heat the oil to 300 degrees F (medium). Cook the potatoes in 3 or 4 batches, frying each for about 3 to 4 minutes. You don't want them to brown, just to be cooked through and slightly soft. Be sure the oil comes back up to temperature between batches. Use a spider or slotted spoon to transfer the fries to a paper towel–lined baking sheet.

- Turn the heat up until the oil reaches 375 to 400 degrees F. Add the fries in batches back into the oil and cook for a few minutes, or until golden brown. Transfer back to the paper towel–lined baking sheet and sprinkle immediately with za'atar and sea salt. Serve with the aioli.

> NOTE: You can also bake the fries in an oven. Preheat the oven to 450 degrees F. Once you have cut, soaked, and dried the potatoes, drizzle with 3 tablespoons olive oil. Spread the potatoes on two baking sheets lined with foil, sprinkle with 1 tablespoon za'atar and sea salt, and bake for 15 minutes. Rotate the baking sheets 180 degrees and bake for 15 to 20 minutes more, or until crisp and golden-brown. Remove from the oven and sprinkle with the remaining 1 tablespoon za'atar and sea salt and serve with the aioli.

CHINESE FIVE-SPICE CHICKEN WINGS WITH CHILI-GARLIC SAUCE

These wings turn out saucy and full of flavor. They disappear quickly, so make sure everyone is gathered around before putting the platter down. These wings get their addictive quality from just the right balance of hot and sweet. Serve them with yogurt dipping sauce and Crispy Jicama and Watermelon Salad with Sumac (page 114), which offers a nice way to cool the palate after eating something spicy.

MAKES 6 TO 8 SERVINGS AS AN APPETIZER

FOR THE CHICKEN.
3 pounds chicken
    wings

FOR THE RUB:
3 tablespoons brown
    sugar
2 tablespoons ground
    Chinese five-spice
1 teaspoon kosher salt

FOR THE SAUCE:
¼ cup orange juice
3 tablespoons honey
3 tablespoons brown
    sugar
2 tablespoons rice
    wine vinegar
2 tablespoons chili garlic
    sauce (we recommend
    Lee Kum Kee)

2 tablespoons black
    bean garlic sauce
2 teaspoons lemon-
    grass paste
    (optional)
2 tablespoons freshly
    squeezed lime juice
½ teaspoon ground
    Chinese five-spice

- Preheat the oven to 500 degrees F.

- Rinse the wings under cool water and pat dry.

- To make the rub, in a small bowl, combine the brown sugar, Chinese five-spice, and salt.

continued

- Spread the wings out on a lightly oiled foil-lined baking sheet. Sprinkle the rub over both sides of the chicken and work it into the skin with your hands. Bake for 10 minutes. Using tongs, turn the wings over and cook for 10 minutes more, until fully cooked and the skin is crispy.

- To make the sauce, in a small bowl, combine the orange juice, honey, brown sugar, vinegar, chili and black bean sauces, lemongrass paste, lime juice, and Chinese five-spice and stir well.

- Heat a 10- to 12-inch skillet over medium heat. Add half of the sauce and cook until it begins to caramelize. Add half of the wings, tossing with a spatula or wooden spoon to coat. Turn down the heat and continue to stir until the chicken is well coated with the sauce, adding 1 to 2 tablespoons water to the pan so the sauce will adhere to the chicken. Transfer to a plate and cover loosely with foil. Add the rest of the sauce and wings and cook in the same manner. Serve on a large platter.

Soups & Stews

Heirloom Tomato Gazpacho
with Urfa Biber 79

Corn Chowder with Chanterelles,
Bacon, and Za'atar 81

Crimson Beet and Apple
Soup with Za'atar Cream 83

Golden Butternut Squash
Soup with Besar 85

Creamy Cauliflower and Leek
Soup with Tikka Masala 88

Sausage, White Bean, and
Kale Soup with Besar 89

Udon Noodle Bowl with
Prawns in Star Anise Broth 91

Spicy Chili with Berbere 92

Parsnip and Potato Soup
with Poudre de Colombo 93

Fisherman's Stew with Harissa 95

HEIRLOOM TOMATO GAZPACHO WITH URFA BIBER

———

This is by far the best gazpacho we have ever tasted, and it's healthy too. The freshness of summer's bounty shines through with a host of seasonal vegetables and heirloom tomatoes. The urfa biber gives this soup a delicious smoky character, and we love the addition of Cotija cheese for the salty, creamy texture it provides. We love to serve it with paella or just with a nice loaf of bread on a hot day.

MAKES 6 TO 8 SERVINGS

5 fresh tomatillos, hulls removed, rinsed well, or 1 cup canned tomatillos

1 large onion, cut into 8 crescents

4 tablespoons extra-virgin olive oil, divided, plus more for garnish

5 medium heirloom or vine-ripened tomatoes, peeled and coarsely chopped

2 medium cucumbers, peeled, seeded, and coarsely chopped

1 medium red or green bell pepper, seeded and coarsely chopped

1 jalapeño pepper, seeded and coarsely chopped

2 cloves garlic, smashed

1 cup bread crumbs

½ cup water

¼ cup red wine vinegar

2 teaspoons kosher salt

1 tablespoon tomato paste

FOR GARNISH:

2 teaspoons urfa biber

1 avocado, diced

Kernels from 1 ear corn (optional)

¼ cup crumbled Cotija (Mexican cheese) or feta (optional)

½ cup peeled and finely chopped cucumber

2 limes, cut into wedges

Hot sauce

- Preheat the broiler.

- Cut the tomatillos in half and place on a baking sheet, cut side down. Arrange the onion on the baking sheet and drizzle with 2 tablespoons of the olive oil. Place the pan on the second rack down from the broiler and roast for 5 to 7 minutes. Remove from the oven and allow to cool slightly.

continued

- In a large bowl, combine the tomatillos, onion, tomatoes, cucumbers, bell pepper, jalapeño, garlic, and bread crumbs and mix together. Stir in the water, vinegar, and salt. Ladle 2 cups at a time into a blender and blend until smooth. Transfer each batch to a large bowl. Repeat until all of the mixture is pureed. Whisk in the remaining 2 tablespoons olive oil and tomato paste until fully incorporated.

- Place serving bowls in the refrigerator to chill. Cover the bowl of gazpacho tightly and refrigerate for 2 hours, or until well chilled. To serve, ladle the soup into the chilled bowls and sprinkle a little urfa biber onto each portion. Serve with all of the garnishes, letting guests choose their favorites.

CORN CHOWDER WITH CHANTERELLES, BACON & ZA'ATAR

The smokiness of the bacon with sweet corn and earthy mushrooms makes for a heavenly combination, which you'll taste when you make this chowder—and the addition of Israeli za'atar takes it to even greater heights! We love cornbread with this chowder, but oyster crackers are great too.

MAKES 6 SERVINGS

3 tablespoons butter, divided

1 tablespoon extra-virgin olive oil

2 leeks, white part only, cleaned and cut into ¼-inch slices

1 cup finely chopped celery

1 fennel bulb, white part only, trimmed and cut into small dice

Kernels from 6 ears corn, or 6 cups frozen kernels, thawed

2 teaspoons Israeli za'atar, divided

5 cups chicken broth

3 medium Yukon Gold potatoes, peeled and cut into small dice

1 bay leaf

1 cup heavy cream or half-and-half (optional)

Sea salt and freshly ground black pepper

6 slices thick bacon, diced, for garnish

2 cups chanterelle, hedgehog, or cremini mushrooms, cleaned and cut into 1-inch pieces

½ teaspoon fresh thyme leaves

◆ In a 5½-quart Dutch oven, heat 2 tablespoons of the butter and olive oil over medium-low. Stir in the leeks and celery and cook until softened. Add the fennel, corn, and 1 teaspoon of the za'atar and cook for 10 minutes. Add the chicken broth and bring to a boil. Immediately reduce the heat to low. Puree half of the soup and return to the pot. Add the potatoes and bay leaf and cook for another 15 minutes. Add the cream and cook another 5 minutes, or until the potatoes are tender. Discard the bay leaf. Season to taste with salt and pepper.

continued

- Meanwhile, in a medium sauté pan, cook the bacon until crisp. Transfer to a plate lined with paper towels to drain. Wipe out the pan, then cook the mushrooms until their moisture releases. Add the remaining 2 tablespoons butter, reduce the heat to medium-low, and continue to cook for 3 minutes. Add the thyme and the remaining 1 teaspoon za'atar and cook, stirring occasionally, until the mushrooms are golden and crisp at the edges. Season lightly with salt and pepper and set aside.

- Serve the chowder in shallow bowls, topping each serving with 1 tablespoon bacon and 2 tablespoons mushrooms.

NOTE: If you're using fresh corn, add 2 to 3 of the cobs to the pot for added flavor—just be sure to remove them before pureeing. In the summer, we love to top this chowder with fresh Dungeness crab or lobster.

CRIMSON BEET & APPLE SOUP WITH ZA'ATAR CREAM

⸻ ❧ ⸻

This enticing crimson soup gets its beauty from the beets. Even better, it is low in fat and very healthy. Its deep purple color makes for a festive addition to any table. The sumac and sesame seeds in the za'atar add just the right seasoning to make this soup so flavorful. If you like more tart flavors, use Syrian za'atar, and for more herbaceous notes, choose the Israeli. Serve with a citrus and fennel salad.

MAKES 4 TO 6 SERVINGS

FOR THE CREAM:
½ cup sour cream or low-fat yogurt
1 tablespoon water
½ teaspoon Israeli or Syrian za'atar

FOR THE SOUP:
6 to 8 medium beets, scrubbed and trimmed

2 tablespoons extra-virgin olive oil
1 teaspoon Israeli or Syrian za'atar
½ yellow onion, diced
2 cups beet greens, rinsed and finely chopped
¼ cup orange juice

1 skin-on apple, coarsely chopped
½ cup water
2 teaspoons freshly squeezed lemon juice

- To make the za'atar cream, mix the sour cream, water, and za'atar together in a small bowl. Cover and refrigerate until the soup is ready.

- To make the soup, cut the beets in half lengthwise. Place the beets in a medium pot and add enough water to cover them. Bring to a boil and cook for 15 minutes. Remove the beets with a slotted spoon to a bowl to cool. Over a large bowl, pour the beet liquid through a fine mesh sieve lined with cheesecloth. Reserve the liquid and discard the cheesecloth and any solids. Once the beets are cool enough to handle, peel and grate them using the large holes of a cheese grater.

continued

- In the same pot over medium-low heat, add the olive oil and za'atar and cook for 2 minutes. Add the onion and cook until sweating and softened, about 5 minutes. Add the strained beet liquid and grated beets back to the pot. Bring to a boil and then reduce to a simmer. Add the beet greens and orange juice and return to a boil; reduce the heat and simmer for 10 minutes.

- Combine the apple, water, and lemon juice in a small bowl. Drain just before garnishing the soup.

- To serve, ladle the soup into bowls and top with a drizzle of the za'atar cream. Sprinkle each serving with 2 tablespoons of the apple garnish. Serve with a crusty French baguette or rye bread and salted butter.

GOLDEN BUTTERNUT SQUASH SOUP WITH BESAR

———— ••• ————

This is a delicious fall soup. We love the taste of the besar with coconut and squash. The ham hock adds a smoky, salty element and the pomegranate garnish gives a bright pop of flavor to the finish. Serve with flatbread or your favorite rustic bread.

MAKES 6 TO 8 SERVINGS

1 tablespoon extra-virgin
  olive oil
1 tablespoon butter
1 leek, cleaned and cut
  into ¼-inch slices
½ yellow onion, diced
1 tablespoon peeled
  and finely grated
  fresh ginger
2 teaspoons ground
  besar

3 medium butternut
  squash, peeled and
  cut into 2-inch cubes
  (about 12 cups)
4 cups chicken or
  vegetable broth
¼ cup apple juice or
  cider
½ cup coconut milk
  (with some of the
  thick cream)

1 ham hock (optional)
1 bay leaf
½ cup heavy cream
Kosher salt and freshly
  ground black pepper
¼ cup crème fraîche or
  coconut cream, for
  garnish
Pomegranate seeds,
  for garnish

◆ In a 5½-quart Dutch oven, heat the olive oil and butter over medium heat. Add the leek and onion and cook for 5 minutes, or until softened. Add the ginger and besar; stir for 1 minute. Add the squash, chicken broth, and apple juice and bring to a slight boil. Stir in the coconut milk. Add the ham hock and bay leaf and bring to a boil over medium-high heat, then reduce the heat, cover, and simmer over low heat for 30 minutes.

continued

- Transfer the ham hock to a bowl and allow to cool. Discard the bay leaf. Remove the soup from the heat and cool slightly. Puree most of the soup with an immersion blender or carefully process in batches in a blender.

- After most of the soup is pureed, add the cream and simmer for 10 minutes. Pull the meat off the ham hock, chop it into small pieces, and return to the pot. Discard the bone. Season to taste with salt and pepper. Ladle the soup into warm bowls and garnish each serving with a drizzle of crème fraîche (if it's too thick to drizzle, thin it with a little water or broth) and garnish with 2 teaspoons pomegranate seeds.

CREAMY CAULIFLOWER & LEEK SOUP WITH TIKKA MASALA

This is a wonderful fall soup and it's really easy to make. You can add cream, but the soup doesn't really need it because once the cauliflower is pureed, you'll think cream has been added! The garnish of apples, walnuts, and bacon give the soup texture and sweetness.

MAKES 4 TO 6 SERVINGS

2 tablespoons extra-virgin olive oil

2 tablespoons butter

2 teaspoons ground tikka masala, divided

2 leeks (white parts only), cleaned and cut into 2-inch pieces

1 head cauliflower, cored, florets cut into 2-inch pieces

½ teaspoon kosher salt

6 cups chicken or vegetable broth, or water

Sea salt

½ Pink Lady, Jona-gold, or Honeycrisp

apple, peeled, cored, and diced, for garnish

½ cup Irresistible Spiced Nuts (page 71), for serving

4 strips cooked bacon, crumbled, for garnish (optional)

- Melt the olive oil and butter in a 5½-quart Dutch oven or heavy pot over medium-low heat. Add 1 teaspoon tikka masala and stir. Add the leeks and sauté, stirring often, for 5 minutes. Add the cauliflower and kosher salt; cook, gently tossing, for 3 minutes. Add the chicken broth and bring to a boil over medium-high heat. Reduce the heat, cover, and simmer for about 30 minutes, or until the cauliflower can be mashed easily on the side of the pan with the back of a fork.

- Remove the soup from the heat and cool slightly. Puree the soup with an immersion blender or carefully process in batches in a blender. Season to taste with sea salt and the remaining 1 teaspoon tikka masala. Return the soup to a simmer. Ladle into warm bowls and garnish with the apple, nuts, and bacon. Serve with a favorite crusty bread.

SAUSAGE, WHITE BEAN & KALE SOUP WITH BESAR

———— ••• ————

The mild and mysterious combination of cinnamon and chile in the besar makes a complement to the vegetables, sausage, and beans. You can also add a cup of fire-roasted diced tomatoes (we recommend Muir Glen). If you want a little more heat, double the urfa biber garnish or include some in the soup pot. Its smoky tobacco flavor helps to round out this soup nicely. Serve with a rustic crusty bread.

MAKES 6 SERVINGS

1 tablespoon extra-virgin olive oil

½ pound andouille or kielbasa sausage (about 2 links), halved lengthwise and cut crosswise into ½-inch slices

2 cups peeled, diced Yukon Gold potatoes

2 carrots, peeled and diced

1 cup chopped yellow onion

2 cloves garlic, chopped

2 teaspoons ground besar, divided

6 cups chicken broth

1 (14.5-ounce) can cannellini beans, rinsed and drained

1 bunch kale, washed, center ribs removed, and roughly chopped

Kosher salt and freshly ground black pepper

½ teaspoon urfa biber or Aleppo pepper flakes

- Heat the olive oil in a 5½-quart Dutch oven over medium heat. Add the sausage and sauté on one side until golden, then flip over and brown the other side. Transfer to a plate. In the same pot, add the potatoes, carrots, onion, garlic, and 1 teaspoon of the besar; sauté briefly. Add the chicken broth and bring just to a boil. Turn the heat down to low and simmer for about 20 minutes, or until the potatoes and carrots are soft.

- Add the sausage, beans, and kale and simmer for 15 minutes. Add the remaining 1 teaspoon besar and cook for 5 minutes more. Season to taste with salt, pepper, and urfa biber. Serve in shallow soup bowls.

UDON NOODLE BOWL WITH PRAWNS IN STAR ANISE BROTH

———— ❖ ————

Udon soup is often just what the doctor ordered. We've infused whole spices into the broth to carry the flavors and included a healthy dose of chiles alongside fresh garnishes to top everything off. The longer you steep the whole spices in the broth, the more flavorful it will be. We like to serve this with Sriracha and hoisin sauce.

MAKES 4 TO 5 SERVINGS

6 cups chicken broth

2 (¼-inch) pieces fresh ginger, sliced lengthwise

1 clove garlic, smashed

2 star anise

1 cinnamon stick

2 cloves

1 bay leaf, cracked but intact

1 pound fresh udon noodles

½ white onion, cut into ¼-inch slices

1 pound medium prawns, peeled and deveined, tails intact

¼ pound snow peas, cut in half diagonally

¼ pound firm tofu, cut into ½-inch cubes

½ cup enoki mushrooms

FOR GARNISH:

¼ cup finely sliced green onion

1 bird chile, thinly sliced

1 lime, cut into wedges

6 sprigs fresh mint

8 to 10 sprigs cilantro

♦ Combine the chicken broth, ginger, garlic, star anise, cinnamon, cloves, and bay leaf into a large stockpot and simmer for 30 minutes. Strain the broth into a large bowl, discarding all of the solids. Return the broth to the pot.

♦ Put the noodles in a colander and run hot water over them to separate and warm. Add the noodles and onion to the broth and bring to a boil over medium-high heat. Turn the heat down to medium-low and add the prawns, snow peas, and tofu, cooking for 2 minutes. Add the mushrooms and cook for 3 minutes.

♦ Ladle the soup into warm bowls, making sure the ingredients are divided evenly. Serve alongside small bowls of the garnishes at the table for guests to add.

SPICY CHILI WITH BERBERE

The berbere makes this chili so delicious—it's got just the right amount of heat and spice. For a different twist on the standard bowl of chili, you can pour it into a cast-iron skillet and top it with Amanda's Cumin-Crusted Cornbread (page 179) batter. Bake at 375 degrees F for 25 minutes and you'll have the best chili pie! You can use harissa instead of berbere to make a smokier flavor profile, or baharat to tone down the heat.

MAKES 8 SERVINGS

2 tablespoons canola oil

1 onion, finely chopped

1 red bell pepper, seeded and chopped

4 cloves garlic, chopped

¼ cup butter, at room temperature

2 pounds beef chuck roast, trimmed and coarsely chopped into ½-inch pieces

1 pound pork shoulder, trimmed and coarsely chopped into ½-inch pieces

1 (15-ounce) can pinto beans, rinsed and drained

¼ cup ground berbere

1 (28-ounce) can fire-roasted diced tomatoes with juice (we recommend Muir Glen)

2 tablespoons fine corn flour (semolina or masa)

Kosher salt and freshly ground black pepper

FOR GARNISH:

Sour cream

1 cup grated medium-sharp cheddar cheese

¼ cup chopped green onion

- Heat the canola oil in a 5- to 6-quart Dutch oven over medium heat, and then add the onion, bell pepper, and garlic. Sauté for 5 minutes, stirring often. Add the butter and let it melt. Add the beef and pork a handful at a time, stirring continuously for 5 minutes. Add the beans and berbere and mix well. Stir in the tomatoes with juice.

- Wrap the pot lid with a kitchen towel to prevent excess liquid from dripping back into the pot and toughening the meat. Secure the towel ends at the top and cover the pot. Simmer over low heat for 2 hours. Stir in the corn flour and cook for 15 minutes longer. Season to taste with salt and pepper. Serve with the sour cream, cheese, and green onion.

PARSNIP & POTATO SOUP WITH POUDRE DE COLOMBO

This soup has a wonderful, velvety texture and the flavors from the poudre de Colombo work in balance with the parsnips and potatoes. You do not need cream to make this soup silky smooth: pureeing the vegetables gives it this effect naturally!

MAKES 8 SERVINGS

1 tablespoon extra-virgin olive oil

1 tablespoon butter

2 tablespoons ground poudre de Colombo

3 large leeks (white and pale green parts only), cleaned and finely chopped

2 pounds parsnips, peeled, cored, and cut into 1-inch cubes

2 pounds Yukon Gold potatoes, peeled and coarsely chopped

3 cups low-sodium chicken or vegetable broth

2 cups water

¼ cup apple juice

Sea salt (preferably fleur de sel)

4 strips cooked bacon, crumbled, for garnish

• In a 4½-quart Dutch oven over medium-low heat, add the olive oil, butter, poudre de Colombo, and leeks; sauté until softened, about 3 minutes. Add the parsnips, potatoes, chicken broth, water, and apple juice and bring to a boil. Turn the heat down to maintain a simmer. Cover and cook for about 20 minutes, or until vegetables are soft. Transfer to a large bowl and allow to cool slightly.

• Add the soup a few cups at a time to a blender or food processor and puree until smooth. Transfer the soup back into the pot in batches; repeat until all of the soup is pureed. Reheat the soup, season to taste with sea salt, and ladle into bowls. Garnish with the crumbled bacon.

> NOTE: If the soup becomes too thick, add more water or broth. If you prefer it with more chunks of vegetables, only puree half of the soup.

FISHERMAN'S STEW
WITH HARISSA

This is a great seafood stew to make any time of the year. Serve it with a green salad and warm rustic bread. The harissa gives this stew the perfect amount of heat without overpowering the seafood.

MAKES 6 SERVINGS

¼ cup extra-virgin olive oil

1 cup finely chopped onion

2 small red bell peppers, seeded and finely chopped

1 tablespoon finely chopped garlic

1 strip thick-cut bacon, cut into 1-inch pieces

2 teaspoons ground harissa

6 medium tomatoes, peeled, seeded, and finely chopped

(or fire-roasted diced tomatoes; we recommend Muir Glen)

1 bay leaf, crumbled

1 large pinch saffron threads, crushed in a mortar and pestle

1 teaspoon kosher salt

1 teaspoon freshly ground black pepper

3 cups fish or chicken broth, or water

½ cup dry white wine

1 tablespoon freshly squeezed lemon juice

16 mussels, scrubbed and debearded

16 small clams, scrubbed

16 large raw shrimp, peeled and deveined, tails intact

½ pound sea scallops, halved

2 tablespoons roughly chopped Italian parsley

1 lemon, cut into wedges, for garnish

- In a 6- to 8-quart Dutch oven, heat the olive oil over medium-high heat. Add the onion, red pepper, and garlic; cook for 5 minutes, stirring frequently, or until the vegetables are soft but not brown. Stir in the bacon and harissa and cook for 2 minutes. Add the tomatoes, bay leaf, saffron, salt, and pepper and cook until

continued

most of the liquid in the pot evaporates and the mixture is thick enough to hold its shape lightly in a spoon.

- Add the fish broth, wine, and lemon juice and bring to a boil. Stir thoroughly, then add the mussels and clams. Cover the pot tightly and reduce the heat to medium; cook for 10 minutes. Add the shrimp and scallops, cover, and cook 5 minutes longer.

- Discard any clams or mussels that do not open. To serve, sprinkle the stew with parsley, taste for seasoning, and ladle into bowls, passing the lemon wedges on the side.

Vegetables & Grains

Roasted Beet Salad
with Watercress and
Dukkah Goat Cheese 99

Crisp Oven-Roasted Broccoli
with Lemon and Harissa 101

Summer Tomato Salad
with Arugula and Urfa Biber 103

Bubble and Squeak
with Poudre de Colombo 105

Vegetable Bread Salad
with Za'atar 107

Honey-Glazed Eggplant
with Ras el Hanout 109

Quinoa with Grilled Vegetables
and Kashmiri Dressing 112

Crispy Jicama and Watermelon
Salad with Sumac 114

Kale Tabbouleh with
Pomegranate Seeds and
Ras el Hanout Dressing 117

Five-Seed Roasted Potatoes 118

Potato and Spinach Roll-Ups
with Poudre de Colombo 119

ROASTED BEET SALAD WITH WATERCRESS & DUKKAH GOAT CHEESE

Roasted beets are dressed with sweet citrus flavors to complement the nutty dukkah and creamy goat cheese. These are served on a bed of watercress for a delightful salad that is refreshing and unique.

MAKES 4 TO 6 SERVINGS

FOR THE BEETS:
1 pound red beets, scrubbed and trimmed
1 pound golden beets, scrubbed and trimmed
¼ cup extra-virgin olive oil
¼ cup orange juice
½ teaspoon kosher salt
Freshly ground black pepper

FOR THE DRESSING:
¼ cup orange juice
2 tablespoons walnut or extra-virgin olive oil
1 tablespoon pomegranate molasses
1 tablespoon honey

FOR THE SALAD:
2 tablespoons dukkah, plus more for garnish
3 ounces goat cheese
2 bunches watercress, larger stems removed
2 oranges, peeled and sectioned
Sea salt

◆ Preheat the oven to 350 degrees F.

◆ To prepare the beets, in a large bowl, toss the beets with the olive oil, orange juice, salt, and pepper. Transfer to a 9-by-13-inch baking dish, cover with foil, and roast for 50 to 60 minutes, or until the beets are tender.

◆ Transfer the beets to a large plate or cutting board to cool slightly, reserving the liquid in the baking dish. Peel the beets once they are cool enough to handle. Cut the smaller beets into 4 wedges and the larger ones into 8 wedges. Transfer them to a large bowl.

continued

- To make the dressing, whisk together the orange juice, walnut oil, pomegranate molasses, and honey in a small bowl. Pour the dressing over the beets and marinate for 30 minutes, tossing occasionally.

- Spread the dukkah on a plate or small baking sheet. Roll the goat cheese in the dukkah, pressing it lightly into the cheese. Break the goat cheese into large chunks.

- Arrange the watercress in a shallow bowl and, with a slotted spoon, scatter the beets and oranges over the top. Drizzle with the dressing and then scatter the goat cheese over the top. Sprinkle with additional dukkah and sea salt and serve.

CRISP OVEN-ROASTED BROCCOLI WITH LEMON & HARISSA

This simple side dish is a great accompaniment for just about anything! We love to take something tried and true, like broccoli, and give it a whole new expression with the addition of spices, and that's just what we've done here. When you slice the broccoli into strips, you allow it to crisp up and have a completely different texture than regular whole florets. To top it off, the harissa and lemon zest give big flavor to this humble vegetable.

MAKES 8 SERVINGS

1 large head broccoli, rinsed, trimmed, and patted dry

¼ cup extra-virgin olive oil

Zest of 1 lemon

1 tablespoon freshly squeezed lemon juice

2 teaspoons ground harissa

1 teaspoon kosher salt

Freshly ground black pepper

• Preheat the oven to 425 degrees F.

• Lightly peel the broccoli stalk. Keeping the stalk and florets intact, slice the florets and stalk where they naturally want to break off. Cut into ½-inch strips, turning the broccoli head and slicing strips as you go, while keeping the floret and stalk together as much as possible.

• Spread the broccoli on a baking sheet and drizzle with the olive oil, lemon zest, lemon juice, harissa, salt, and pepper and toss to coat. Bake for 15 to 20 minutes, or until the florets start to become lightly golden and crispy on the edges. Serve immediately.

SUMMER TOMATO SALAD
WITH ARUGULA & URFA BIBER

There's nothing better than having a variety of tomatoes growing in your garden—maybe the very best are those sweet little cherry tomatoes right when you pick them. If you can't get heirlooms, try to find the tomatoes that are still attached to the vine. The small yellow pear tomatoes are also delicious. When fresh corn is in season, cut it right off the cob and add the kernels to this salad.

MAKES 6 SERVINGS

FOR THE DRESSING:
2 tablespoons minced
    shallot
2 tablespoons freshly
    squeezed lemon juice
2 teaspoons sugar
¼ cup extra-virgin
    olive or walnut oil
Kosher salt and freshly
    ground black pepper

FOR THE CHIVE OIL:
1 cup chopped chives
⅓ cup extra-virgin olive
    or grapeseed oil

FOR THE SALAD:
2 pounds heirloom
    or red and yellow
    cherry tomatoes
3 cups lightly packed
    fresh arugula
8 fresh basil leaves, thin-
    ly sliced (chiffonade)

FOR GARNISH:
6 strips cooked bacon,
    crumbled
¼ cup shaved
    Manchego or
    Parmesan or crum-
    bled feta cheese
1 tablespoon urfa biber
2 tablespoons chive oil
Fleur de sel and freshly
    ground black pepper

♦ To make the dressing, combine the shallot, lemon juice, and sugar in a medium bowl. Drizzle in the olive oil 1 teaspoon at a time, whisking constantly. After adding 4 teaspoons, pour in the rest of the olive oil very slowly, whisking constantly. Season to taste with salt and pepper.

continued

- To make the chive oil, combine the chives and olive oil in a blender and blend until smooth. Strain through a fine mesh sieve lined with cheesecloth. Discard the solids. The oil can be refrigerated for up to 1 week.

- To make the salad, cut any large tomatoes into wedges and cherry tomatoes in half and transfer to a large bowl. Put the arugula and basil into another large bowl. Drizzle with half of the dressing and toss. Gently toss the rest of the dressing with the tomatoes; sprinkle with the bacon, Manchego, and urfa biber. Spoon the tomato mixture over the arugula. Drizzle with chive oil and season with sea salt and pepper.

BUBBLE & SQUEAK
WITH POUDRE DE COLOMBO

——— ••• ———

Bubble and squeak is a dish traditionally made with leftovers. During the eighteenth century, it was most often made with meat and cabbage, but our version boasts a hearty combination of potatoes and brussels sprouts—perfect winter fare. The poudre de Colombo really brightens up this dish, but you can also try besar.

MAKES 6 TO 8 SERVINGS

2 pounds medium russet potatoes (about 4 large) or 4 to 5 Yukon Gold potatoes, peeled and halved

½ cup milk, warmed

3 tablespoons butter, at room temperature

3 tablespoons sour cream

Kosher salt and freshly ground black pepper

½ pound brussels sprouts

4 tablespoons butter or extra-virgin olive oil, divided

2 leeks (white parts only), halved and cut into ½-inch slices

½ yellow onion, finely chopped

2 teaspoons ground poudre de Colombo

• Put the potatoes in a medium pot and fill with enough water to cover. Bring the water to a boil and cook until they can be easily pierced with a fork. Drain and cool slightly.

• Transfer the warm potatoes to a large bowl and mash with a potato masher or ricer. Add the milk, butter, and sour cream. Continue to mash until almost smooth. Season to taste with salt and pepper.

continued

- Fill a pot halfway with water and bring to a boil. Add the brussels sprouts and cook until bright green and tender, about 8 to 10 minutes. Drain and cut into ¼-inch slices.

- In a 10- to 12-inch cast-iron or other nonstick skillet, melt 2 tablespoons of the butter over medium-low heat. Add the leeks, onion, and poudre de Colombo and sauté until soft and translucent. Add the brussels sprouts and cook, stirring, for 5 minutes. Add the mashed potatoes and gently fold them into the vegetables until well combined. Press down on the mixture, smoothing out the top. Cook for about 10 minutes, undisturbed, until the bottom surface is golden brown.

- Remove the skillet from the heat. Position a plate a little larger than the skillet upside down on top. Holding both the plate and skillet tightly, flip the whole thing over in one swift move. The potato cake should come right out onto the plate.

- Add the remaining 2 tablespoons butter to the skillet and swirl until melted. Slide the cake back into the skillet over medium heat and cook for about 10 minutes, or until the second side is also golden brown. Cut into wedges and serve.

> NOTE: You can add kale, parsnips, sweet potatoes, or other favorite vegetables you have on hand; the options are endless. Bubble and squeak also makes a great breakfast served with a fried or poached egg on top and your favorite hot sauce.

VEGETABLE BREAD SALAD WITH ZA'ATAR

———— ❦ ————

Bread salad is such a comfort dish, with satisfying bits of seasoned bread and intense flavors in every bite from the anchovies, olives, mustard, and spices. This is a nice accompaniment to roast chicken or grilled salmon, and you can use either Israeli or Syrian za'atar to suit your tastes. We also like to toss in urfa biber or Aleppo pepper if we are in the mood for a little heat.

MAKES 4 SERVINGS

FOR THE BREAD:

⅓ cup extra-virgin olive oil

2 cloves garlic, finely minced

2 teaspoons Israeli or Syrian za'atar

Kosher salt and freshly ground black pepper

1 loaf of rustic Italian bread, such as ciabatta, cut into 1-inch cubes (about 8 cups)

FOR THE DRESSING:

3 anchovies

1 clove garlic

¼ cup red wine vinegar

1 tablespoon Dijon mustard

2 tablespoons freshly squeezed lemon juice

⅓ cup extra-virgin olive oil

Freshly ground black pepper

FOR THE SALAD:

1 small red onion

2 medium heirloom or other tomatoes, cut into 1-inch cubes

1 English cucumber, cut into 1-inch slices and quartered

½ cup pitted picholine or kalamata olives, halved

2 teaspoons Israeli or Syrian za'atar

Sea salt

7 mint leaves, thinly sliced (chiffonade), for garnish

¼ cup basil leaves, thinly sliced (chiffonade), for garnish

- Preheat the broiler.

- To make the bread cubes, combine the olive oil, garlic, za'atar, and salt in a large bowl and let sit for 5 minutes. Toss the bread cubes in the mixture until well

continued

coated. Spread the cubes on a baking sheet and position 6 to 7 inches from the broiler. Broil for 4 minutes, or until lightly toasted. Remove from oven, turn the bread cubes over, and broil for 4 minutes more. Remove from the oven, turn down the heat to 300 degrees F, and bake for 5 minutes. Set aside to cool and crisp up.

- To make the dressing, in a blender, combine the anchovies, garlic, vinegar, Dijon, and lemon juice; blend for a few seconds. Slowly add the olive oil and blend for 10 seconds more. Season with pepper to taste.

- To assemble the salad, combine the bread, onion, tomatoes, cucumber, and olives in a large serving bowl. Drizzle with the dressing and toss to coat. Sprinkle with za'atar and sea salt. Garnish with the mint and basil and serve.

HONEY-GLAZED EGGPLANT
WITH RAS EL HANOUT

◆••◆

This dish is often the first to go at our summer barbecues; it's a great way to change the minds of people who "don't like eggplant." Pillowy poufs of grilled eggplant are coated with a glaze of honey, oil, and spice that crisps up perfectly on the outside. Ras el hanout imparts subtle floral notes alongside cinnamon, nutmeg, and hints of pepper that dance delightfully on the tongue.

MAKES 4 TO 6 SERVINGS

½ cup honey

½ cup extra-virgin olive oil

¼ cup white wine vinegar

1 tablespoon ground ras el hanout

½ teaspoon flake or kosher salt

4 firm young eggplants

Needles from 2 sprigs fresh rosemary, finely chopped, for garnish

- In a large bowl, whisk together the honey, olive oil, vinegar, ras el hanout, and salt.

- Rinse the eggplants and slice them on a slight angle into 1-inch rounds. Lay the rounds on a cutting board and make a few shallow slits into the flesh on each side.

- Toss the eggplant with the honey mixture to coat. Let the eggplant sit at room temperature for about 1 hour, tossing occasionally.

- Prepare a charcoal grill for medium-hot coals or preheat a gas grill to medium-high. Oil the grate.

continued

- Arrange the eggplant slices on the oiled grill. Brush the top with honey glaze from the bowl and cook for about 7 minutes, or until you can see the purple skin changing color about halfway up the slices. Turn the slices over and brush again with the glaze. Cook until the slices are tender all the way through and charred to perfection. Mind your grill carefully throughout cooking as the eggplant can burn quickly if the grill is too hot.

- Arrange the eggplant on a platter and drizzle with any remaining glaze. Sprinkle rosemary over the top. Serve hot.

> NOTE: The versatile honey glaze can be used on other grilled vegetables, like zucchini, yellow squash, peppers, and onions, or for even more variety—switch up the spice! Try substituting baharat, besar, or Kashmiri garam masala for the ras el hanout.

QUINOA WITH GRILLED VEGETABLES & KASHMIRI DRESSING

⬧

Quinoa is a fluffy whole grain with a fabulous texture and loads of nutrition—some even call it a "super food"—and it is super quick and easy to cook. It is a perfect blank slate for flavor, and that's where our Kashmiri curry dressing comes in—the quinoa just soaks it up. Yum! The roasted flavors from the grilled vegetables are the perfect match.

MAKES 6 TO 8 SERVINGS

FOR THE DRESSING:
- ¼ cup orange juice
- 2 tablespoons freshly squeezed lemon juice
- 1 tablespoon finely minced shallot
- 1 tablespoon honey
- 1 teaspoon ground Kashmiri curry
- ¼ cup extra-virgin olive or grapeseed oil
- Kosher salt and freshly ground black pepper

FOR THE QUINOA:
- 4 tablespoons extra-virgin olive oil
- 2 cups quinoa
- 3½ cups vegetable broth
- 2¼ teaspoons kosher salt, plus more for seasoning
- 1 Walla Walla sweet onion, cut into 3-inch crescents
- 2 baby zucchini, ends trimmed, cut lengthwise into quarters

- ½ bunch asparagus, ends trimmed
- 1 teaspoon ground Kashmiri curry
- Zest of 1 lemon
- Freshly ground black pepper
- ¼ cup crumbled feta cheese, for garnish
- Small handful mint leaves, thinly sliced (chiffonade), for garnish

⬧ To make the dressing, in a small bowl, combine the orange juice, lemon juice, shallot, honey, and Kashmiri curry. Slowly whisk in the olive oil, season with salt and pepper to taste, and set aside.

⬧ In a 3½-quart Dutch oven or medium saucepan over medium-high heat, heat 1 tablespoon of the olive oil. Add the quinoa and cook, stirring, until lightly toasted, about 2 minutes. Add the vegetable broth and salt and bring to a boil. Reduce the heat to low, cover, and simmer until the quinoa is tender and all of the liquid is absorbed, about 15 minutes. Fluff with a fork and set aside to cool.

+ Heat an outdoor grill to medium-high heat or preheat the broiler.

+ Meanwhile, prepare the vegetables. Spread the onion, zucchini, and asparagus on a baking sheet. Drizzle with the remaining 3 tablespoons olive oil. Sprinkle with the Kashmiri curry, lemon zest, salt, and pepper. Turn the vegetables so they're evenly coated with the oil and spices.

+ Transfer the vegetables to a large piece of foil (or use a vegetable basket, if you have one) and set on the grill. Alternatively place the baking sheet under the broiler to roast. Cook until the vegetables start to turn golden. For thin asparagus, cook for about 4 minutes; for thicker asparagus, cook for another 2 to 3 minutes. When all of the vegetables have nice color and have been turned a few times with tongs, remove from the heat.

+ Chop the grilled vegetables into ½-inch pieces. Combine the grilled vegetables with the quinoa, drizzle with the dressing, and toss gently. Sprinkle with the feta and fresh mint, season to taste with more salt, pepper, and Kashmiri curry and serve.

CRISPY JICAMA & WATERMELON SALAD WITH SUMAC

This crisp salad of jicama and watermelon with citrus, sumac, and mint is very refreshing on a hot summer day. Jicama, like radishes, is always better when you add it to a bowl of ice water after slicing—it makes a world of difference in its crispness and texture. Many different spices can be used in place of sumac if you want to try something different—Aleppo and urfa can add a little heat, nigella seeds make a decorative and crunchy addition, or you can garnish with a flaky finishing salt.

MAKES 6 TO 8 SERVINGS

FOR THE SALAD:
1 medium jicama, peeled and cut into ½-inch slices, then cut into matchsticks
Ice water, to cover
Juice of ½ lime
½ small seedless watermelon, cut into 2-inch cubes (about 4 cups)
1 cup blueberries

FOR THE DRESSING:
2 tablespoons freshly squeezed lime juice
2 tablespoons grapeseed or canola oil
1 tablespoon honey

FOR GARNISH:
3 tablespoons crumbled Cotija or feta cheese (optional)
1 tablespoon very thinly sliced mint leaves
⅛ teaspoon sumac
Kosher salt and freshly ground black pepper

- In a large bowl, cover the jicama with the water. And the lime juice and set aside.

- In another large bowl, combine the watermelon and blueberries. Drain the jicama and spread the pieces on several layers of paper towels; pat dry. Add the jicama to the watermelon and blueberries.

- To make the dressing, whisk together the lime juice, oil, and honey in a small bowl.

- Drizzle the dressing over the fruit. Sprinkle with the cotija, mint, and sumac. Season to taste with salt and pepper. Gently toss with your hands to prevent mashing the watermelon and serve.

KALE TABBOULEH
WITH POMEGRANATE SEEDS &
RAS EL HANOUT DRESSING

This refreshing salad is perfect holiday fare. At a time when greens can often be over-shadowed by sweets, put this on the table and it will become everyone's first choice instead. The bright citrus vinaigrette helps tenderize the kale, and the pomegranate seeds add a sunny pop of festive flavor.

MAKES 6 SERVINGS

FOR THE BULGUR:
1 cup bulgur wheat or
   quinoa

FOR THE DRESSING:
3 tablespoons freshly
   squeezed lemon
   juice
3 tablespoons orange juice
2 teaspoons honey
2 tablespoons red wine
   vinegar
1 shallot, minced

2 teaspoons ground ras
   el hanout
1 teaspoon kosher salt
⅓ cup extra-virgin olive
   or walnut oil

FOR THE SALAD:
1 bunch Tuscan
   (Lacinato) kale, large
   ribs removed, leaves
   finely chopped
Seeds from 1
   pomegranate

1 apple, cut into ½-inch
   cubes
¼ cup finely chopped
   fresh parsley
3 tablespoons thinly
   sliced fresh mint
   leaves
3 tablespoons thinly
   sliced fresh basil leaves
½ teaspoon fine sea salt
Freshly ground black
   pepper

- Cook the bulgur or quinoa according to package instructions. Set aside to cool.

- To make the dressing, whisk together the lemon juice, orange juice, honey, vinegar, shallot, ras el hanout, and salt in a small bowl. Slowly whisk in the oil.

- In a large bowl, combine the kale and dressing and toss to coat. Add the bulgur, pomegranate seeds, apple, parsley, mint, basil, salt, and pepper and toss again. Let sit for 10 minutes to allow the flavors to meld and then serve.

FIVE-SEED ROASTED POTATOES

This aromatic adaptation of Bengali five-spice first came to us from chef Jerry Traunfeld of Poppy restaurant in Seattle, and we never tire of mixing up the salt-and-seed combinations to try a new version. The satisfying explosion of crunch and flavor when you bite into the seeds makes these potatoes a pleasing side for roasted meats or breakfast eggs.

MAKES 6 SERVINGS

2 pounds small red or fingerling potatoes, halved	1 teaspoon brown mustard seed	½ teaspoon ajwain seed
2 tablespoons extra-virgin olive oil	1 teaspoon nigella seed	½ teaspoon fennel seed
	1 teaspoon cumin seed	1 teaspoon flake or kosher salt, divided

◆ Preheat the oven to 425 degrees F.

◆ Put the potatoes into a large pot over medium-high heat and fill with enough water to cover. Bring the water to a boil and cook the potatoes for 5 to 8 minutes, or until tender.

◆ In a cast-iron skillet over medium heat, combine the olive oil, mustard, nigella, cumin, ajwain, and fennel seeds. Toast in the oil until the seeds begin to pop and sputter.

◆ In a large bowl, toss the potatoes, spices, and ½ teaspoon of the salt until evenly coated. Spread the seeded potatoes on a baking sheet and roast for 20 to 30 minutes, or until golden and crisp on the outside. Sprinkle with the remaining ½ teaspoon salt and serve.

POTATO & SPINACH ROLL-UPS WITH POUDRE DE COLOMBO

The wonderful blend of turmeric, coriander, and fenugreek really shine through in this recipe. You can substitute the flour tortillas with Pogacha Flatbread with Sea Salt and Dukkah (page 59) or simply serve the curry mixture over rice.

MAKES 5 TO 6 SERVINGS

4 cups lightly packed fresh spinach, large stems removed

4 tablespoons extra-virgin olive oil or Niter Kibbeh Spiced Butter (page 219), divided

1 yellow or white onion, finely chopped

2 cloves garlic, minced

½ jalapeño pepper, seeded and finely diced

2 teaspoons finely minced peeled fresh ginger

1½ tablespoons ground poudre de Colombo

¼ teaspoon ground cinnamon

5 large russet potatoes, peeled and cut into 1-inch cubes

1 (15-ounce) can garbanzo beans, drained and rinsed

1 large carrot, peeled and cut into small dice

1½ cups chicken both

6 tablespoons coconut milk

1 tablespoon brown sugar

½ teaspoon kosher salt

3 tablespoons chopped fresh cilantro (optional)

5 to 6 large flour tortillas (plain or spinach)

Sliced fresh pineapple, for serving

Steamed rice, for serving

* Fill a small pot with water and bring to a boil. Add the spinach and cook for 10 seconds. Drain in a colander. Run a little cold water over the spinach, then squeeze out excess water. Dry the spinach by pressing it between several layers of paper towels. Coarsely chop the spinach and set aside.

continued

- In a large sauté pan, heat 2 tablespoons of the olive oil over medium heat. Add the onion, garlic, jalapeño, and ginger and cook for 3 minutes, or just until the onions are soft and translucent. Sprinkle with the poudre de Colombo and cinnamon and cook for 2 more minutes. Add the potatoes and cook for 3 minutes, stirring to coat with the spices. Add the garbanzo beans, carrot, chicken broth, coconut milk (for extra creaminess, include some of the thick cream at the top of the can), brown sugar, and salt; cover and cook over low heat for 20 minutes, then remove the lid and cook for 20 more minutes. Add the spinach and cook 5 minutes more, or until the potatoes and carrots are tender. Remove from the heat and sprinkle with the cilantro.

- Brush each side of the tortillas lightly with the remaining 2 tablespoons olive oil. Heat a 10- to 12-inch cast-iron skillet over medium heat. Add one tortilla and cook until lightly golden. Flip and brown the other side. Transfer the cooked tortillas to a plate in a stack.

- Place 1 tortilla on a serving plate and, using a slotted spoon, spoon on 6 table-spoons of the curry mixture. Fold the ends up and then pull the sides over to meet in the center (like an envelope). Serve with the pineapple and rice.

> NOTE: We like to add 2 to 3 cardamom pods or 2 tablespoons coconut cream to the rice before steaming for extra flavor.

Shellfish & Seafood

Dukkah-Encrusted
Seared Scallops 123

Steamed True Cod
with Harissa-Garlic Sauce 125

Grilled Salmon with Za'atar
and Sauce Gribiche 127

Halibut Poached in Olive
Oil with Saffron 130

Dungeness Crab Melts
with Kashmiri Curry 133

Pan-Fried Sole with Berbere
and Lemon Butter 135

Coconut-Steamed Mussels
with Tikka Masala 137

Skillet Prawns
with Poudre de Colombo 138

Oyster Po' Boys with Harissa
and Muffuletta 141

Pan-Roasted Halibut
with Kashmiri Garam
Masala Glaze 143

Shellfish Paella with Harissa
and Urfa Biber 145

Spicy Shrimp and Grits 147

DUKKAH-ENCRUSTED SEARED SCALLOPS

The dukkah makes a perfect crust with its hints of coriander, thyme, and hazelnut. You can even use it on salmon, swordfish, and tuna. Serving the scallops on a bed of parsnip puree with chanterelles makes it almost too good to be true.

MAKES 4 SERVINGS

FOR THE PUREE:

4 to 5 medium parsnips, peeled, ends trimmed

¼ cup apple juice or cider

3 tablespoons heavy cream

Kosher salt

FOR THE MUSHROOMS:

2 tablespoons extra-virgin olive oil, divided

2 tablespoons butter, divided

1 medium leek (white parts only), cleaned, halved lengthwise, and cut into ¼-inch slices

½ pound chanterelle mushrooms, cleaned, trimmed, and quartered

1 teaspoon fresh thyme leaves

Kosher salt and freshly ground black pepper

FOR THE SCALLOPS:

¼ cup coarsely ground dukkah

12 large sea scallops, side-muscle removed

2 tablespoons extra-virgin olive oil, plus more for brushing

¼ teaspoon kosher salt

1 tablespoon fresh thyme leaves, for garnish

- To make the puree, first cut the parsnips in half lengthwise and then cut into 2-inch pieces. Put them in a 4-quart saucepan, cover with water, and bring to a boil. Cook for 10 to 15 minutes, or until the parsnips are easy to mash with the back of a fork. Drain and transfer to a blender with the apple juice. Blend until smooth, adding a little water if the mixture is thick. Transfer the puree to a small saucepan and warm over low heat. Swirl in the cream and season with salt to taste. Turn off the heat and cover.

- To prepare the mushrooms, in a 10- to 12-inch skillet, melt 1 tablespoon each of the olive oil and butter over medium heat. Add the leeks and sauté briefly

continued

until soft and just starting to brown. Transfer to a plate. In the same pan, add the remaining 1 tablespoon olive oil and butter. Add the mushrooms and sauté for 3 to 4 minutes. Sprinkle with the thyme and continue to cook for 8 to 10 minutes more, or until the mushrooms are dark brown around the edges (lower the heat if the mushrooms are browning too quickly). Season with salt and pepper. Transfer to the plate with the leeks, cover with foil to keep warm, and set aside.

• Preheat the oven to 250 degrees F. Meanwhile, rewarm the parsnip puree over low heat, stirring occasionally.

• To prepare the scallops, spread the dukkah on a plate. Lightly brush the scallops with olive oil and sprinkle with just a pinch of salt, then press the scallops into the dukkah, coating the tops and bottoms. Transfer to a plate. Heat the olive oil in a 10- to 12-inch skillet over medium-high heat. Once hot, add the scallops, dukkah-side down, taking care not to crowd the pan (do this in two or three batches). Cook the scallops for about 3 to 4 minutes without moving, then use tongs to flip them over. They should release easily once a crust has formed. Cook for 3 to 4 minutes more.

• Remove the scallops from the pan, spread them on a baking sheet, and place them in the warm oven. Add the leeks and mushrooms to the skillet and warm briefly over medium-low heat. Place ¼ to ½ cup parsnip puree on each plate. Remove the scallops from the oven and place 3 each on top of the puree with one-quarter of the leeks and mushrooms. Season with sea salt to taste and sprinkle with the thyme. Serve immediately.

> TIP: When buying scallops, be sure to ask for dry-packed scallops without any additives. If they are wet-packed, they have an additive called sodium tripolyphosphate (STPP), which is not our preferred type.

STEAMED TRUE COD
WITH HARISSA-GARLIC SAUCE

Do you ever wonder what to do with that jar of fermented black beans sitting in your refrigerator? Well, this recipe will have you not only using your black bean sauce, it will also inspire you to use it in many other applications. It's simply great with green beans, braised bok choy, or on all types of seafood. The harissa gives this dish a balancing heat. You can use any white fish, just note that it takes longer for thicker fillets to cook.

MAKES 4 SERVINGS

1 clove garlic, minced

2 tablespoons extra-virgin olive oil

2 teaspoons ground harissa

3 tablespoons black bean–garlic sauce (we recommend Lee Kum Kee)

1 tablespoon rice wine vinegar

2 teaspoons honey

4 (4- to 6-ounce) true cod fillets

1 large (or 4 small) bok choy, rinsed and cut into 2-inch slices

1 tablespoon soy sauce

4 medium green onions (green parts only), thinly sliced

2 tablespoons chopped fresh cilantro

Steamed rice, for serving

♦ In a mortar and pestle (or a small bowl with a fork), combine the garlic, olive oil, and harissa. Mash together until they form a smooth paste. In a medium bowl, whisk together the harissa paste, black bean sauce, vinegar, and honey until they form a sauce.

♦ Place a steamer basket in a large pot of hot water that comes up the sides about 2 inches. Cover the pot and bring to a boil over medium-high heat. Arrange the fillets in the steamer basket and spoon 1 tablespoon of the harissa mixture over each fillet. Cover and steam over medium heat for about 6 minutes, or until the fish turns white and starts to flake. Remove from heat and set aside.

continued

- In a nonstick skillet, combine the bok choy and soy sauce and toss. Cover and cook for 3 minutes. Toss again and continue to cook until all the liquid is absorbed and the white part of the bok choy is tender. Remove from the heat, cover, and set aside.

- Pour the remaining sauce over the fish and sprinkle with the green onions and cilantro. Serve with the bok choy and rice.

GRILLED SALMON WITH ZA'ATAR & SAUCE GRIBICHE

The tart flavor from the sumac in the Syrian za'atar goes perfectly with the salmon but Israeli za'atar also works well. The sauce gribiche (an herb-caper sauce) is a lighter substitute for tartar sauce. It is delicious served alongside the salmon with a platter of grilled asparagus.

MAKES 6 SERVINGS

FOR THE SAUCE:
1 hard-boiled egg, finely chopped
¼ cup mayonnaise
¼ cup sour cream
2 tablespoons finely diced red onion
2 tablespoons finely diced cornichons
2 tablespoons finely chopped tarragon
2 tablespoons finely chopped parsley
1 tablespoon capers, drained
1 tablespoon freshly squeezed lemon juice
1 tablespoon red wine vinegar
1 teaspoon fresh or dried dill, (optional)

FOR THE ASPARAGUS:
1 to 2 bunches asparagus (about 30 spears), trimmed
3 tablespoons extra-virgin olive or walnut oil
1 teaspoon lemon zest
1 teaspoon sumac (or more lemon zest)
½ teaspoon smoked or sea salt
¼ teaspoon freshly ground black pepper

FOR THE SALMON:
6 (6-ounce) skin-on salmon fillets, each about 1-inch thick
3 tablespoons extra-virgin olive oil
¼ cup Syrian za'atar
2 tablespoons brown sugar
1 teaspoon lemon zest
½ teaspoon kosher salt
¼ teaspoon freshly ground black pepper

◆ To make the sauce gribiche, in a medium bowl, combine all of the sauce ingredients and mix until blended well. Set aside.

continued

- To prepare the asparagus, spread the asparagus out over a foil-lined baking sheet. Drizzle with the olive oil, then sprinkle with the lemon zest, sumac, salt, and pepper. Toss to coat and set aside.

- Preheat the broiler to high. Position an oven rack at the second notch from the top.

- To prepare the salmon, place each piece skin side down on a foil-lined baking sheet. Fold up the edges of the foil slightly. Rub the fillets with olive oil. In a small bowl, stir together the za'atar, brown sugar, lemon zest, salt, and pepper. Sprinkle about 1 tablespoon of the spice rub on each fillet.

- Heat a charcoal or gas grill to medium-high. Using tongs, lay the asparagus spears perpendicular to the grate. Grill the asparagus for about 3 minutes, or until they begin to brown. Turn with tongs and cook for about 4 minutes more; transfer to a platter and keep warm.

- Place the salmon on foil on the grill. Cook for 4 to 5 minutes. Transfer the salmon back to the baking sheet and place it under the oven broiler for 3 to 4 minutes, or until the top of the salmon starts to caramelize.

- Serve the salmon and asparagus with the sauce gribiche and a nice rustic bread or flatbread.

> NOTE: If you are grilling sockeye, it will cook in about half the time of wild king salmon. Finishing the fish under the broiler helps it cook and enables the salmon to caramelize.

HALIBUT POACHED IN OLIVE OIL WITH SAFFRON

When I was enrolled in a course at the Culinary Institute of America in Napa Valley, I had the great honor of taking a class with David Tanis. He taught us how to poach halibut in olive oil and then turn that oil into an aioli. For this recipe, I've added lemon, bay leaf, saffron, and garlic. This gives even more flavor to the fish and aioli. You could try using star anise as well.

MAKES 4 SERVINGS

3 cups extra-virgin olive oil

3 cloves garlic, smashed

1 lemon, cut into ¼-inch slices

1 fresh or dried bay leaf, broken but still intact

3 star anise

¼ teaspoon saffron, ground in a mortar and pestle

4 (6- to 7-ounce) halibut fillets or steaks, each about 1-inch thick

1 large coddled egg

Juice from ½ lemon

Kosher salt

• Preheat the oven to 225 degrees F.

• Put the olive oil in a 10-inch ovenproof sauce pan. Place over low heat until the oil is about 120 degrees F (check with a thermometer). Add the garlic, lemon slices, bay leaf, star anise, and saffron; let the flavors infuse for 3 minutes. Carefully slip the halibut into the oil, leaving space around each fillet. If you need more oil to cover the fish, add a little. Transfer the pan to the oven and bake for 20 to 25 minutes. Remove from the oven very carefully.

• Reserve 1 cup of the oil. Put the coddled egg and lemon juice into a blender. Blend, slowly adding the reserved oil, until it thickens and starts to resemble aioli. Using a slotted spoon, remove the fish from the pan to a platter. Season to taste with salt and serve the aioli alongside the fish (or put a dollop on top).

DUNGENESS CRAB MELTS WITH KASHMIRI CURRY

⸻

It's not every day you catch fresh Dungeness crab, but if you have a chance to drop crab pots and collect these amazingly tasty creatures, then this is a great recipe to have. If you cannot get crab, you can use baby shrimp or a combination of both. The warm, aromatic spicing of the Kashmiri curry complements the crab without overpowering its delicate flavor.

MAKE 6 OPEN-FACED SANDWICHES

4 tablespoons butter, at room temperature, or extra-virgin olive oil

3 brioche rolls or English muffins, halved

1 Honeycrisp, Gala, or Jonagold apple, peeled and finely diced

¼ cup finely diced celery

¼ cup finely diced red onion

¼ jalapeño pepper, seeded and minced (optional)

1 medium lemon, zested (about 1 teaspoon) and juiced (about 2 tablespoons)

3 tablespoons mayonnaise

2 teaspoons ground Kashmiri curry

Freshly ground black pepper

1 pound cooked fresh crabmeat

¾ cup grated Gruyère cheese

- Preheat the broiler to medium-high.

- Lightly spread the butter on each half of the brioche and place them on a baking sheet. Broil, watching carefully—remove as soon as they turn light golden brown; set aside, leaving the broiler on.

continued

- Combine the apple, celery, onion, jalapeño, lemon zest and juice, mayonnaise, Kashmiri curry, and pepper into a large bowl. Mix until blended, then gently fold in the crabmeat.

- Spoon ⅓ cup of the crab on each brioche, then top with 2 tablespoons of Gruyère. Broil just until the cheese is melted and lightly golden. Serve with a lightly dressed watercress or mixed green salad.

PAN-FRIED SOLE WITH BERBERE & LEMON BUTTER

——— •◆• ———

Sole is a great fish that too often gets dismissed. It is so easy to cook, and pan-frying is a favorite method. The fish gets a beautiful crust and the berbere adds a nice kick! The nuttiness of the browned butter (known as beurre noisette*) and lemon also complements the spice. Serve with a nice pinot gris or Sancerre.*

MAKES 4 SERVINGS

FOR THE BUTTER:

4 tablespoons unsalted butter

Juice of ½ lemon, strained of any pulp

Kosher salt and freshly ground black pepper

FOR THE FISH:

1 cup hazelnuts, toasted and outer skins removed

1½ cups all-purpose flour, for dredging

1 tablespoon ground berbere

½ teaspoon kosher salt

¼ teaspoon freshly ground black pepper

2 eggs, beaten

½ cup milk

8 (4-ounce) skinned sole fillets (or substitute true cod)

2 tablespoons butter

2 tablespoons vegetable oil

3 tablespoons roughly chopped parsley, for garnish

1 lemon, cut into wedges, for garnish

◆ To make the lemon butter, melt the butter in a small saucepan over medium-low heat. Continue heating until it turns a golden-brown color. Add the lemon juice and a pinch of salt and pepper. Remove from the heat and set aside.

◆ Preheat the oven to 250 degrees F. Line a baking sheet with foil.

◆ Put the hazelnuts in a blender and process until finely ground with just a bit of texture.

continued

◆ In a flat casserole or pie dish, combine the flour, berbere, salt, and pepper. In a medium bowl, whisk together the eggs and milk. Spread the ground hazelnuts on a plate. Lightly dredge the sole fillets one at a time in the spiced flour, shaking off the excess. Then coat with the egg mixture and press both sides in the ground hazelnuts.

◆ Heat a 12-inch skillet over medium-low heat and melt the butter and vegetable oil. Cook 2 fillets at a time for 2 to 3 minutes per side, or until golden. Transfer to the baking sheet and place in the oven to keep warm. Repeat with the remaining fillets (you can put some plates into the oven at this time to warm them).

◆ Gently rewarm the lemon butter over low heat.

◆ Place 2 fillets on each warmed plate. Drizzle a little lemon butter over each fillet and garnish with the parsley and a lemon wedge. Serve with Five-Seed Roasted Potatoes (page 118).

COCONUT-STEAMED MUSSELS WITH TIKKA MASALA

———◆◆◆———

Mussels have become easier to prepare these days, a fact that's due to the way they are grown. Mussel producers, such as our local Penn Cove Shellfish, use a machine that debeards the mussels, making it a huge time saver for the consumer. Just keep in mind that once debearded, they are very perishable. We just love the flavor of mussels and curry. You could also use white fish or scallops with this delicious broth.

MAKES 6 TO 8 SERVINGS

2 tablespoons extra-virgin olive oil

½ yellow onion, diced

1 minced shallot

2 teaspoons ground tikka masala

½ cup coconut milk

¼ cup chicken broth

2½-inch piece fresh ginger, cut into ¼-inch slices

1 tablespoon fish sauce (optional)

1 stalk lemongrass (white parts only) or 2 tablespoons

freshly squeezed lemon juice

2 to 3 pounds mussels, scrubbed and de-bearded

Juice of ½ lime

Sriracha sauce (optional)

• Heat the olive oil in a 10- to 12-inch skillet over medium-low heat. Add the onion and shallot and cook for 3 to 4 minutes. Add the tikka masala and stir, then add the coconut milk, chicken broth, ginger, and fish sauce. Bring to a slight boil over medium-high heat, then reduce to medium-low. Cut the lemongrass in half lengthwise and smash it with the side of a knife to release its oils. Add the crushed stalks to the broth.

• Add the mussels (discard any mussels that don't close when tapped on the counter or that have cracked shells). Cover and cook for 5 minutes, or until the shells open and the meat inside is firm. Squeeze with the lime juice and serve. Serve with crusty bread or rice; if you'd prefer a little more heat, drizzle with Sriracha.

SKILLET PRAWNS
WITH POUDRE DE COLOMBO

————◆————

If you like heat, use harissa or berbere in place of the poudre de Colombo, as they are great options with prawns. You can also try using Niter Kibbeh Spiced Butter (page 219) instead of the regular butter—it will only add more flavor! Serve the prawns with steamed rice.

MAKES 4 SERVINGS

FOR THE VEGETABLES:
2 tablespoons butter
2 fennel bulbs, trimmed, halved, and cut into ½-inch slices
1 large yellow onion, halved and cut into ½-inch slices
1 cup chicken broth
1 tablespoon Pernod, or ½ teaspoon fennel seed, smashed

FOR THE PRAWNS:
2 teaspoons ground poudre de Colombo
1 teaspoon Hungarian paprika
2 teaspoons lemon zest
1 teaspoon fresh thyme leaves
1 teaspoon brown sugar
⅛ teaspoon kosher salt
2 tablespoons butter
2 tablespoons extra-virgin olive oil

2 cloves garlic, minced
1 pound medium prawns (about 18-24), peeled and deveined, tails intact
2 tablespoons freshly squeezed lemon juice
Chopped fresh parsley, for garnish

◆ To prepare the vegetables, in a 12-inch stainless steel skillet, melt the butter. Add the fennel and onion and cook for 4 minutes, flip, and cook for 4 minutes more. Add the chicken broth and Pernod; cover and cook for about 15 minutes, or until the onion is soft. Uncover and cook until all of the liquid has evaporated and the fennel and onion begin to brown. Remove from the heat and cover to keep warm.

- Meanwhile, to prepare the prawns, in a small bowl, mix together the poudre de Colombo, paprika, lemon zest, thyme, sugar, and salt. In a 10- to 12-inch skillet, melt the butter and olive oil over medium-low heat. Add the garlic and cook for 1 minute. Add the spice mixture and the prawns and cook for 2 to 3 minutes; flip over and cook for 2 minutes more.

- Rewarm the fennel mixture over medium-low heat.

- Spoon one-quarter of the mixture onto each plate and top with 4 to 5 prawns. Sprinkle over the lemon juice, garnish with the parsley, and serve.

OYSTER PO' BOYS
WITH HARISSA & MUFFULETTA

———•◆•———

We love a good oyster po' boy. You'll need to have the perfect roll—one that's not too crispy, holds together, and won't get soggy. We like a French bread roll lightly toasted and buttered. The olive salad gives this po' boy a New Orleans twist. In this recipe, the kick is in the breading, and of course you have to serve it with Crystal brand hot sauce!

MAKES 6 SANDWICHES

FOR THE SPREAD:
½ cup jarred or homemade muffuletta olive salad
1 cup mayonnaise

FOR THE SLAW:
2 cups thinly sliced purple cabbage
2 cups thinly sliced Napa or Savoy cabbage
1 Honeycrisp, Fuji, or Pink Lady apple, cored and thinly sliced, then cut into matchsticks
½ fennel bulb, thinly sliced

¼ cup orange juice
¼ cup apple cider vinegar
¼ teaspoon kosher salt

FOR THE OYSTERS:
2 large eggs
½ cup buttermilk
2 tablespoons hot sauce
30 small oysters, shucked and drained (unrinsed)
1½ cups fine-medium cornmeal
½ cup all-purpose flour or finely crushed saltines

1 tablespoon ground harissa or Creole seasoning
2 teaspoons kosher salt
1 teaspoon freshly ground black pepper
½ teaspoon smoked paprika
2 baguettes, cut into thirds, or 6 French bread rolls
⅓ cup softened butter or extra-virgin olive oil
Canola oil, for frying
Lime wedges, for serving

- To make the spread, add the olive salad to a blender and blend until almost a paste. Using a spatula, transfer the paste to a small bowl. Stir in the mayonnaise until well combined.

- To make the slaw, combine the cabbage, apple, fennel, orange juice, vinegar, and salt in a large bowl and toss well. Set aside.

continued

- Preheat the broiler.

- In a medium bowl, whisk together the eggs, buttermilk, and hot sauce. Add the oysters; cover and refrigerate for 10 minutes.

- In another medium bowl, whisk together the cornmeal, flour, harissa, salt, pepper, and paprika.

- Cut the baguettes in half lengthwise and spread the inside with 1 tablespoon butter or lightly brush with olive oil. Arrange on a baking sheet. Place on the second oven rack down and broil until lightly golden brown. Set aside.

- Turn the oven temperature down to 250 degrees F.

- Heat the canola oil in a 3½- to 4-quart Dutch oven (the oil should come up the sides at least 1½ inches) over medium-high heat to 350 degrees F. Using a slotted spoon, drain about 4 to 5 oysters. Dredge the oysters in the cornmeal mixture until well coated, shaking off any excess. Transfer to a plate and repeat with the remaining oysters. Fry 8 to 10 oysters at a time in the hot oil for about 3 minutes. Transfer to a paper towel–lined baking sheet.

- Place the baking sheet in the oven to keep warm and repeat with the rest of the oysters. Once all of the oysters are fried, place the rolls on a platter and smear 2 tablespoons of the spread on each side. Add ½ cup slaw to the top of the bun and 4 to 5 oysters to the bottom. Serve with lime wedges and hot sauce.

NOTE: The best oysters are available in the months that have an R in them. You can shuck your own oysters for this recipe or buy them pre-shucked in jars at most seafood counters. Look for the extra-small size.

PAN-ROASTED HALIBUT WITH KASHMIRI GARAM MASALA GLAZE

We recommend making the spiced oil ahead of time and having it on hand. I like to buy organic virgin coconut oil from Trader Joe's, but you should be able to find a comparable brand in most grocery stores (usually in the natural section). It's worth the cost—especially for this use. This dish is great served with white jasmine rice—you can even swirl in 1 tablespoon spiced oil to give the rice extra flavor.

MAKES 4 SERVINGS

FOR THE SPICED OIL:

2 cups virgin coconut oil

½ yellow or white onion, finely diced

1 tablespoon minced garlic

2 teaspoons minced peeled fresh ginger

1 tablespoon ground Kashmiri garam masala

½ teaspoon turmeric

¼ teaspoon kosher salt

FOR THE GLAZE:

½ fennel bulb, cored and cut into small dice

½ cup apple cider

6 tablespoons chicken or vegetable broth

¼ cup dry white wine

1 teaspoon Pernod

3 sprigs fresh thyme

1 Pink Lady, Jonagold, or Honeycrisp apple, peeled and finely diced

FOR THE FISH:

4 (7-ounce) halibut fillets or steaks

Kosher salt and freshly ground black pepper

♦ To make the spiced oil, heat a heavy medium saucepan over medium heat and melt the coconut oil. (Place the jar in a bowl of warm water first if you need to liquefy the oil in order to measure.) Once melted, add the onion, garlic, ginger, garam masala, and turmeric. Turn down the heat to low and simmer for 10 minutes. Add the salt and simmer for 5 minutes. Turn off heat and let the mixture

continued

sit, allowing the flavors to infuse for 15 minutes. Line a fine mesh strainer with several layers of slightly damp cheesecloth and set over a bowl. Pour the oil through. Strain again until it is clear. You can store the oil in an airtight container in the refrigerator for up to 6 months.

- To make the glaze, in a small saucepan, combine the fennel, apple cider, chicken broth, wine, Pernod, and thyme; bring to a boil. Turn down the heat to medium-high and cook until the liquid is reduced by half. Stir in the apple, cooking just to warm. Set aside.

- Preheat the oven to 350 degrees F.

- Season the halibut lightly with salt and pepper. In a large ovenproof skillet, heat 1 tablespoon of the spiced oil. Add the halibut and cook until a crust forms and the fillets release naturally from the pan, 4 to 5 minutes. Add 3 tablespoons of the spiced oil to the pan with the glaze and warm over low heat. Turn the fillets over and baste with the warmed glaze. Transfer the skillet to the oven and cook the halibut for 8 to 10 minutes, or until opaque.

- Remove the skillet from the oven. Serve the halibut on a bed of rice and drizzle each fillet with 2 tablespoons of the glaze.

SHELLFISH PAELLA
WITH HARISSA & URFA BIBER

———— ••• ————

This classic dish from Spain provides the perfect background for Northwest shellfish. The saffron gives the whole dish a beautiful golden color, and the addition of harissa gives it the little extra heat and flavor it needs. There are so many variations of paella—you can feature chicken, sausage, and any kind of shellfish, along with beans, artichoke hearts, or other vegetables. This is our favorite version.

MAKES 8 SERVINGS

6 tablespoons extra-virgin olive oil, divided

½ cup diced onion

2 cloves garlic, minced

1 medium red bell pepper, seeded and cut into ¼-by-1½-inch strips

1 large tomato, peeled, seeded, and finely chopped, or 1 cup canned fire-roasted diced tomatoes, drained (we recommend Muir Glen)

1 tablespoon ground harissa

1 pound mussels, scrubbed and debearded

1 pound clams, scrubbed

1 pound medium prawns, peeled and deveined, tails intact

6 cups chicken broth or water

½ pound firm, pre-cooked chorizo or other smoky-hot sausage cut into 1-inch slices

3 cups short-grain paella rice, such as Bomba or Valenciano

1 teaspoon kosher salt

½ teaspoon smoked paprika

½ teaspoon urfa biber

¼ teaspoon saffron threads, ground in a mortar and pestle

½ cup frozen peas, thawed

1 tablespoon chopped fresh parsley, for garnish

2 lemons, cut into wedges, for serving

• Preheat the oven to 400 degrees F.

• Heat 4 tablespoons of the olive oil in a 12-inch paella pan over medium-high heat. Add the onion, garlic, bell pepper, tomato, and harissa. Cook, stirring often,

continued

for about 10 minutes. Lower the heat to medium and continue to cook until the mixture forms into a thick paste. Transfer the paste to a bowl and set aside.

- Combine the mussels, clams, and prawns in a large bowl and set aside.

- In a medium saucepan, add the chicken broth and bring to a boil. Turn off the heat.

- In a 12- to 14-inch skillet or paella pan over medium heat, add the remaining 2 tablespoons olive oil. Add the sausage and brown for about 2 minutes on each side. Transfer to a plate and set aside. Drain any fat from the skillet. Combine the harissa paste, paella rice, salt, paprika, urfa biber, and saffron in the same skillet; stir to mix. Add the hot chicken broth. Bring to a boil over high heat, stirring constantly. Remove from the heat and tuck all of the shellfish into the rice mixture. The clams and mussels should be hinge side down in the paella so they can open easily. Place the pan on the very bottom rack in the oven and cook for 15 minutes. Do not stir. Sprinkle the peas on top and return to the oven for 10 minutes more, or until all of the liquid has been absorbed and the rice is no longer crunchy. Stir in the cooked sausage. Cover the paella with a dishtowel and let sit for 5 minutes before serving. Garnish with the parsley and serve right out of the pan with lemon wedges on the side.

NOTE: At no point should you stir the paella after it goes in the oven or it will get mushy. When Dungeness crab is in season we like to serve the cooked legs and body meat on the side or on top of the finished paella (along with corn on the cob, of course!).

SPICY SHRIMP & GRITS

We like to use Turkish urfa biber in this dish. It has a smoky-sweet taste, like a sun-dried tomato. This pepper starts out red, and as it dries on the plant, turns a dark burgundy color. The Aleppo pepper, which has more heat, is best added toward the end of cooking to keep it from mellowing too much. We recommend using stone ground or coarse ground cornmeal for the grits.

MAKES 4 SERVINGS

FOR THE SHRIMP:

1 tablespoon extra-virgin olive oil
1 precooked chorizo or andouille sausage, cut into ¼-inch slices
1 pound shrimp, peeled and deveined, tails intact
1 onion, chopped
1 clove garlic, chopped
1 red bell pepper, seeded, cut into thin strips, and halved

1 (14.5-ounce) can fire-roasted diced tomatoes, drained (we recommend Muir Glen)
¼ teaspoon smoked paprika
¼ teaspoon urfa biber
¼ cup heavy cream
½ teaspoon Aleppo pepper
2 teaspoons ground harissa
¼ teaspoon kosher salt

FOR THE GRITS:

3 cups water
3 cups chicken broth
2 cups coarse ground cornmeal
1 tablespoon butter
¼ cup half-and-half
6 tablespoons grated sharp white cheddar
Kosher salt and freshly ground black pepper
¼ cup roughly chopped Italian parsley, for garnish

♦ To prepare the shrimp, heat a 10- to 12-inch cast-iron skillet over medium heat; add the olive oil. Sauté the sausage until golden brown on both sides. Transfer to a plate, leaving any oil in the pan. Add the shrimp and cook for 2 to 3 minutes on each side. Transfer to the plate with the sausage. Add the onion and garlic to the skillet and cook for 2 minutes, stirring occasionally. Add the bell pepper, tomatoes, paprika, and urfa biber and cook over medium-low heat for 15 minutes, or until a thick sauce forms. Add the cream, Aleppo, harissa, and salt; cook for 1 minute. Remove from the heat.

continued

- Meanwhile, to make the grits, bring the water and chicken broth to a boil in a medium saucepan. Slowly add the cornmeal, whisking constantly; once the mixture is boiling again, turn the heat to low and simmer, stirring often, for 20 minutes, or until thick and soft. Add the butter and stir, then stir in the half-and-half. Add the cheese and stir until melted. Season lightly with salt and pepper.

- Reheat the skillet with the sauce over medium heat until hot. Turn the heat down to medium-low, return the sausage and shrimp back to the skillet, and heat for 3 minutes.

- Put 1 cup of the grits on each plate, making a well in the center. Top with about 1 cup of the sauce mixture, being sure to include several shrimp and pieces of sausage. Sprinkle with the parsley and serve.

Meat & Poultry

Seared Rib-Eye Steak
with Baharat 151

Maple-Glazed Pork Chops
with Besar 153

Pork Ribs with Chinese
Five-Spice and
Barbecue Sauce 155

Pork Tenderloin with Ras el
Hanout and Urfa Biber
Sweet Potatoes 158

Braised Beef Short Ribs
with Caramelized Onions
and Baharat 161

Crusted Rack of Lamb
with Syrian Za'atar 163

Brisket with Berbere and
Whiskey Barbecue Sauce 165

Grilled Steak Salad
with Chinese Five-Spice 166

Baked Chicken with
Tikka Masala Sauce 169

Melt-in-Your-Mouth Pot Roast
with Besar and Spaetzle 171

Oven-Roasted Chicken
with Harissa-Honey Glaze 173

Berbere Sloppy Joes 176

SEARED RIB-EYE STEAK
WITH BAHARAT

—◆—

Necessity is the mother of invention, and this beautiful pairing is a classic example. When we found ourselves out of our favorite steak rub one night, we had baharat on hand and whipped this up. Now there is a new favorite in the house. Baharat adds aromatic elements of cinnamon and allspice to a simple meat rub, and it transforms the rib-eye with unexpected flavors. The earthiness of the mushrooms is a nice complement to the spices and steak. We like to serve this with garlic mashed potatoes.

MAKES 6 SERVINGS

FOR THE MUSHROOMS:

2 pounds mixed cremini, chanterelle, and other mushrooms, cleaned and quartered

2 tablespoons butter, divided

2 tablespoons extra-virgin olive oil, divided

2 tablespoons finely minced shallot

2 teaspoons fresh thyme leaves

1 teaspoon kosher salt, divided

½ teaspoon freshly ground black pepper, divided

1 yellow onion, halved and cut into ½-inch slices

FOR THE RUB:

3 tablespoons ground baharat

1½ tablespoons brown sugar

1 teaspoon kosher salt

Freshly ground black pepper

FOR THE STEAK:

1 tablespoon extra-virgin olive oil

3 (1-pound) rib-eye steaks (about 1-inch thick)

◆ Preheat the oven to 375 degrees F.

◆ In a 10- to 12-inch cast-iron skillet over medium heat, add the mushrooms and cook until any moisture from the mushrooms releases and evaporates. Add 1 tablespoon each of the butter and olive oil, and the shallot and cook until the mushrooms start

continued

to crisp up and turn golden. Sprinkle with the thyme, ½ teaspoon of the salt, and ¼ teaspoon of the pepper. Transfer to a plate. In the same skillet, heat the remaining 1 tablespoon each butter and olive oil over medium-low heat. Add the onion and sauté for 30 minutes, stirring gently every 4 to 5 minutes. Turn the heat down to low if the onions are cooking too quickly. Once caramelized, sprinkle with the remaining salt and pepper. Return the mushrooms to the skillet, stir, and set aside.

- To make the rub, stir together the baharat, brown sugar, salt, and pepper in a small bowl. Generously rub the steaks on both sides.

- To prepare the steaks, in a 10- to 12-inch cast-iron skillet, heat the olive oil over medium-high heat. Add the steaks and cook for 3 minutes on each side, or until a nice golden crust forms. Transfer the steaks in the pan to the oven. Continue cooking for 6 minutes for medium-rare. Remove from the oven, loosely cover with foil, and allow the steaks to rest for at least 5 minutes. Reheat the skillet with the mushrooms for several minutes, or until nice and hot. Slice the steaks into ½-inch-thick slices and serve half of a rib-eye to each guest with the mushroom mixture on the side.

MAPLE-GLAZED PORK CHOPS WITH BESAR

———— ◆◆◆ ————

We love brining with apple juice because it imparts sweet flavors into the meat. When you combine that taste with besar and bacon, you can't go wrong! Note that the brining requires you to plan and prepare several hours ahead of serving this dish. Serve with your favorite chunky applesauce or Wirtabel's Melon Chutney (page 208).

MAKES 4 SERVINGS

FOR THE BRINE:
1½ cups apple juice or cider
2 cups water
½ cup brown sugar
¼ cup kosher salt
4 sprigs fresh thyme

2 to 3 sprigs fresh rosemary, pounded lightly with a pestle

FOR THE CHOPS:
4 pork chops
2 tablespoons ground besar

2 tablespoons brown sugar
1 teaspoon kosher salt
4 to 5 strips thick-sliced smoked bacon
1 tablespoon plus 1 teaspoon maple syrup

◆ Combine the apple juice, water, brown sugar, salt, thyme, and rosemary in a medium bowl; stir until the sugar and salt have dissolved. Add the pork chops, making sure they are submerged in the liquid; if not, add a little more water or apple juice. Brine for at least 4 hours and up to 12 hours.

◆ Preheat the oven to 350 degrees F.

◆ In a small bowl, mix together the besar, brown sugar, and salt.

continued

- Remove the pork chops from the brine and rinse with cold water. Dry well with paper towels. Spread 2 teaspoons of the besar mixture on each side of each pork chop. Let them sit for 5 minutes.

- In a 10- to 12-inch cast-iron skillet over medium heat, add the bacon and cook until almost done (some fat uncooked). Transfer to a cutting board and cut each piece in half. Drain all but 1 tablespoon of fat from the skillet. Heat the skillet over medium-high heat and add the pork chops. Cook for 4 to 5 minutes on one side, or until golden brown. Turn over and cook for 4 to 5 more minutes. Turn the chops on their sides to crisp up and brown. Drizzle 1 teaspoon maple syrup on each pork chop. Top with 2 pieces of bacon and place the skillet in the oven for 8 to 10 minutes. Remove from oven, cover loosely with foil, and let rest for several minutes before serving.

PORK RIBS WITH CHINESE FIVE-SPICE & BARBECUE SAUCE

━━━ ••• ━━━

We love to fix ribs in the summertime—really anytime—using this method. Delicious and moist, they just fall off the bone. Chinese five-spice makes the perfect rub for ribs! You can make the sauce ahead of time; just reheat before using.

MAKES 4 SERVINGS

FOR THE SAUCE:
1 tablespoon extra-virgin
    olive oil
1 clove garlic, minced
1 tablespoon minced
    peeled fresh ginger
½ cup hoisin sauce
2 tablespoons ketchup
1 tablespoon soy sauce

1 tablespoon
    Worcestershire sauce
1 tablespoon apple
    cider vinegar

FOR THE RIBS:
3 tablespoons ground
    Chinese five-spice
3 tablespoons brown
    sugar

1 teaspoon kosher salt
2 racks baby back
    pork ribs (about 4
    pounds total)
2 cups light beer
¼ cup finely chopped
    green onion, for
    garnish

* To make the sauce, in a small saucepan, heat the olive oil over medium-low heat. Add the garlic and ginger and sauté until the oil becomes fragrant, about 2 minutes. Add the hoisin, ketchup, soy sauce, Worcestershire, and vinegar and cook, stirring, for 5 minutes. Remove from the heat and set aside.

* Mix the Chinese five-spice, brown sugar, and salt in a small bowl. Remove the back sinew (the layer of thick white skin) from the ribs. It works best if the ribs are dry: you can get under the sinew with your fingers and pull it off in one strip. Rub both sides of both racks with the spice mixture. Wrap with plastic wrap, place in the refrigerator, and allow to season for 2 hours or up to 1 day.

continued

- Preheat the oven to 325 degrees F.

- Line two baking sheets with heavy-duty foil, both a few inches longer than the rib racks. Place 1 rib rack in the center of each piece of foil. Fold up the ends, making boats out of the foil (they will need to hold 1 cup of liquid each). Crimp the foil together, leaving about a 3-inch opening in the top. Pour 1 cup of the beer into each foil boat. Place the baking sheets in the oven and braise for 2 hours.

- Brush the racks with the sauce. You can serve the ribs like this or finish them on a barbecue for 5 to 10 minutes to get a little charring on the meat. Place extra sauce on the table for guests to add if desired. Sprinkle over the green onions and serve with grilled corn on the cob and Kale Tabbouleh with Pomegranate Seeds and Ras el Hanout Dressing (page 117).

PORK TENDERLOIN WITH RAS EL HANOUT & URFA BIBER SWEET POTATOES

Pork tenderloin needs flavor and it is the perfect background for spice blends. The complex flavors of ras el hanout in the pork rub help to form a crust on the outside, leaving the inside beautifully moist. You'll love the nuttiness the dukkah imparts to the sweet potatoes.

MAKES 4 SERVINGS

FOR THE POTATOES:
2 sweet potatoes, peeled and cut into ½-inch slices
¼ cup butter, melted
¼ cup light brown sugar
⅓ cup apple cider

3 tablespoons maple syrup
½ teaspoon urfa biber
1 tablespoon ground dukkah
Kosher salt

FOR THE PORK:
¼ cup ground ras el hanout

2 tablespoons brown sugar
1 teaspoon kosher salt
2 pork tenderloin (about 1 pound), silver skin removed
4 tablespoons extra-virgin olive oil, divided

- Position a rack in the center of the oven and preheat the oven to 400 degrees F.

- To prepare the potatoes, place the potato slices in a large bowl and drizzle with the melted butter. Add the brown sugar, apple cider, maple syrup, urfa biber, dukkah, and salt. Toss until the potatoes are evenly coated. Spread the potatoes on a baking sheet and pour any liquid on top. Cover with foil and bake for 20 minutes. Remove the foil, and use a spatula to stir the potatoes. Bake, uncovered, for 20 to 25 minutes, or until the potatoes can be easily pierced with a fork and have formed a golden crust. Set aside.

- Lower the oven temperature to 350 degrees F.

- To prepare the pork, in a small bowl, mix together the ras el hanout, brown sugar, and salt. Rub each tenderloin with 1 tablespoon of the olive oil, then coat all over with the spice mixture. Heat a cast-iron skillet over medium-high heat. Add the remaining 2 tablespoons olive oil and, once hot, add the tenderloins and cook, turning, until browned on all sides, about 6 minutes. Place the skillet in the oven and roast, uncovered, for about 20 minutes, or until the center reaches 145 degrees F to 150 degrees F. Remove from the oven, tent loosely with foil, and let rest for 5 minutes.

- Return the sweet potatoes to the oven for ten minutes.

- To serve, cut the tenderloin at an angle into slices about ¾-inch thick. Place the slices back into the skillet and coat with the juices. Serve with the potatoes and a favorite chutney.

BRAISED BEEF SHORT RIBS WITH CARAMELIZED ONIONS & BAHARAT

———◆———

This dish truly is the epitome of comfort food! The baharat raises the bar on braised short ribs. The heat and spice together balance nicely, and the caramelized sweet onions melt in your mouth. Lightly dredging the meat in the spiced flour before searing not only helps to thicken the braising liquid but adds delicious flavor to the meat. We like to do this when making beef stew as well. Adding the bay leaf and the carrots toward the end of cooking will result in a more subtle hint of bay and will prevent overcooking the carrots.

MAKES 6 TO 8 SERVINGS

½ cup all-purpose flour

2 tablespoons ground baharat

1 teaspoon kosher salt

½ teaspoon freshly ground black pepper

4 pounds beef short ribs, excess fat trimmed

3 tablespoons butter

2 tablespoons extra-virgin olive oil

2 sweet onions, cut into ½-inch slices

1 cup beef broth

½ cup ketchup

½ cup beer

2 tablespoons brown sugar

1 tablespoon red wine vinegar

½ teaspoon dry mustard

6 medium carrots, peeled and cut at an angle into 2 inch pieces

1 dried Turkish bay leaf

• Position a rack in the center of the oven and preheat the oven to 350 degrees F.

• In a medium bowl, stir together the flour, baharat, salt, and pepper. Lightly coat the short ribs in the spiced flour. Shake off any excess.

continued

- Heat a 12-inch skillet over medium-high heat; add the butter and olive oil and brown several ribs at a time without crowding the pan. Cook, turning and browning on all sides, for 3 to 4 minutes. Transfer the cooked ribs to a baking sheet. Repeat with the remaining ribs. Reduce the heat to medium-low, add the onion, and cook until soft, about 5 minutes.

- In a 5½-quart Dutch oven, combine the onion and ribs. Add the beef broth, ketchup, beer, brown sugar, vinegar, and dry mustard; cover and braise for 1½ hours.

- Add the carrots and bay leaf, cover, return to the oven, and braise for another hour, or until the meat pulls apart with a fork and the carrots can be easily pierced. Serve over a bed of mashed Yukon Gold potatoes or polenta.

CRUSTED RACK OF LAMB WITH SYRIAN ZA'ATAR

This incredible recipe is as beautiful as it is delicious, and it's a great choice for a spring dinner. Lamb (or any game meat) goes well with Syrian za'atar because of the sumac, coriander, and star anise. Asparagus makes for the perfect accompaniment.

MAKES 4 SERVINGS

FOR THE LAMB:
2 racks domestic lamb, trimmed of fat (about 3 pounds)
Kosher salt and freshly ground black pepper

FOR THE RUB:
2 tablespoons ground Syrian za'atar
1 tablespoon finely chopped fresh rosemary

¼ teaspoon kosher salt
2 tablespoons honey
2 teaspoons freshly squeezed lemon juice
2 cloves garlic, finely chopped

FOR THE ASPARAGUS:
1 bunch asparagus, ends trimmed and bottom 3 inches peeled

1 tablespoon hazelnut or extra-virgin olive oil
1 tablespoon ground dukkah
2 teaspoons lemon zest or sumac
Kosher salt and freshly ground black pepper

- Position a rack in the center of the oven and preheat the oven to 350 degrees F.

- To prepare the lamb, score the fat on the racks, lightly making a crisscross pattern. Season the lamb with salt and pepper. Place the racks in a 12-inch cast-iron skillet, meat side up, interlocking both sets of ribs in the center of the skillet. Cover the bone ends with foil and place the skillet in the oven. Partially close the oven door and bake for 8 to 10 minutes.

- Meanwhile, to prepare the rub, in a small bowl, mix together the za'atar, rosemary, and salt.

continued

- Remove the lamb from the oven and let cool slightly; reduce the temperature to 325 degrees F.

- In a small bowl, mix the honey with the lemon juice. Rub the lamb with the chopped garlic, brush with the honey mixture, then spread the za'atar rub all over on the front and back of the rack, pressing into the meat. Return the skillet to the oven and bake for 20 to 25 minutes.

- Meanwhile, prepare the asparagus. Put a few inches of water in a medium pot with a steamer basket. Add the asparagus, cover, and steam for 6 minutes for thick asparagus and 3 to 4 minutes for thin. Carefully pull out the steamer basket and arrange the asparagus on a platter. Drizzle with the hazelnut oil and sprinkle with the dukkah, lemon zest, salt, and pepper.

- Remove the lamb from the oven, cover loosely with foil, and let rest for 3 to 5 minutes.

- Cut the lamb into chops between the rib bones and serve each guest 3 to 4 chops with several pieces of asparagus.

BRISKET WITH BERBERE
& WHISKEY BARBECUE SAUCE

The unexpected flavors of allspice, ginger, and fenugreek in the berbere nestle right into this down-home brisket, and it boasts both richness and melt-in-your-mouth tenderness. Serve it with Amanda's Cumin-Crusted Cornbread (page 179) and sautéed leafy greens.

MAKES 6 TO 8 SERVINGS

FOR THE SAUCE:
1 clove garlic, smashed
1 tablespoon extra-vir-
    gin olive oil
½ cup whiskey (Jack
    Daniel's and Maker's
    Mark work well)
½ cup orange juice
¼ cup apple cider vinegar
¼ cup maple syrup

1 (6-ounce) can tomato
    paste
1 tablespoon
    Worcestershire
    sauce
1 tablespoon soy sauce
1 teaspoon freshly
    ground black pepper

FOR THE BEEF:
3 tablespoons coarsely
    ground berbere
1 tablespoon brown
    sugar
1 teaspoon kosher salt
1 teaspoon smoked salt
3 pounds beef brisket
2 tablespoons extra-
    virgin olive oil

- Preheat the oven to 300 degrees F.

- To make the whiskey sauce, sauté the garlic in the olive oil in a medium saucepan until fragrant. Add the whiskey, orange juice, vinegar, maple syrup, tomato paste, Worcestershire, soy sauce, and pepper and stir until well blended. Simmer for 5 minutes, remove from the heat, and set aside.

- In a small bowl, whisk together the berbere, brown sugar, and salts. Rub the mixture well into all sides of the brisket.

- In a large cast-iron skillet heat the olive oil over medium heat. Brown the brisket on each side and remove the skillet from the heat. Pour the sauce over the brisket and tightly cover the pan. Bake for about 3 hours, or until the brisket pulls apart with a fork. Allow to rest for 15 minutes before serving.

GRILLED STEAK SALAD WITH CHINESE FIVE-SPICE

—◆—

Steak salad is the perfect summer dinner—slices of flavorful grilled meat on top of the freshest summer greens and vegetables. Bring on the grill! Every cook will appreciate this go-to marinade that never fails. If you want the steak to have really nice flavor, let it marinate for at least 2 hours, but don't exceed 5 hours or it will become too salty and affect the texture of the meat. Sprinkling urfa biber over the tomatoes on the salad packs extra flavor.

MAKES 6 SERVINGS

FOR THE MARINADE:

¼ cup soy sauce

¼ cup orange juice

2 tablespoons canola oil

2 tablespoons rice
   wine vinegar

2 tablespoons honey

1 tablespoon ground
   Chinese five-spice

2 teaspoons sesame oil

2 teaspoons minced
   peeled fresh ginger

1 clove garlic, finely
   chopped

¼ teaspoon crushed
   red pepper flakes

1 teaspoon sesame
   seeds

1½ pounds flank or
   hanger steak

FOR THE DRESSING:

2 tablespoons freshly
   squeezed lemon juice

2 tablespoons honey

1 tablespoon Dijon
   mustard

1 tablespoon minced
   shallot

¼ teaspoon kosher salt

Freshly ground black
   pepper

¼ cup walnut or extra-
   virgin olive oil

FOR THE SALAD:

6 cups baby spinach

2 oranges, peeled and
   sectioned

1 avocado, diced

¼ red onion, thinly sliced

◆ To make the marinade, whisk together the soy sauce, orange juice, canola oil, rice wine vinegar, honey, Chinese five-spice, sesame oil, ginger, garlic, red pepper flakes, and sesame seeds in a large, nonreactive bowl. Pour the marinade into a large zippered bag (or use a glass baking dish and turn the steak over after 1 hour). Add the steak and squeeze out some of the air before sealing. Place in the refrigerator and marinate for at least 2 hours but no more than 5 hours.

- To make the dressing, in a medium bowl, whisk together the lemon juice, honey, Dijon, shallot, salt, and pepper. Slowly drizzle in the walnut oil 1 to 2 tablespoons at a time, whisking constantly. Set aside.

- Preheat the broiler or a grill to medium-high.

- To make the salad, divide the spinach among 6 plates. Scatter the oranges, avocado, and red onion over the top. Set aside.

- Broil the steak for 4 to 5 minutes per side for medium-rare. Transfer to a cutting board, loosely cover with foil, and let rest for 10 minutes. Slice the meat against the grain and divide it among the salads. Drizzle with dressing and serve.

BAKED CHICKEN
WITH TIKKA MASALA SAUCE

————◆◆————

This recipe is so easy if you make the blend ahead of time because you would normally need to add a dozen or more spices. Tikka makes a delicious and quick curry in a hurry! You can add any vegetables, like snow peas or spinach. This dish can be made a day ahead and reheated—it will have even more flavor.

MAKES 6 SERVINGS

1 (15-ounce) can coconut milk, stirred well, divided

3 tablespoons ground tikka masala, divided

3 cloves minced garlic

1 tablespoon finely grated peeled fresh ginger

2 teaspoons kosher salt

2 pounds boneless, skinless chicken breasts, quartered

3 tablespoons coconut oil, or 2 tablespoons butter, or 1 tablespoon extra-virgin olive oil

1 small yellow onion, thinly sliced

3 tablespoons tomato paste

1 (15-ounce) can crushed tomatoes with juice (we recommend Muir Glen)

1 cup chicken broth

¼ cup finely chopped green onion, for garnish

¼ cup fresh cilantro leaves, for garnish

½ cup roasted and salted cashews, for garnish

½ jalapeño, thinly sliced, for garnish

♦ Whisk together 1 cup of the coconut milk, 2 tablespoons of the tikka masala, garlic, ginger, and salt in a large bowl. Add the chicken and toss to coat. Cover and chill for 4 hours.

♦ Heat the coconut oil in a large skillet over medium heat. Add the yellow onion and cook for 3 minutes, stirring. Add the tomato paste and cook until it becomes dark in color. Add the remaining 1 tablespoon tikka masala and cook for 3 to 4 minutes.

continued

Add the tomatoes with juice and cook over medium-low heat for about 8 minutes. Add the chicken broth and the remaining coconut milk; simmer for about 20 minutes.

- Place an oven rack in the top third of the oven and preheat the broiler.

- Spread the chicken on a foil-lined baking sheet. Broil the chicken until it starts to bubble and dark brown spots form, about 10 minutes.

- Remove from the oven and cool slightly. Cut into 1-inch pieces. Add the chicken to the sauce over medium-low heat and cook, stirring occasionally, for 8 minutes, or until the chicken is cooked through. Garnish with the green onion, cilantro, cashews, and jalapeño; serve with steamed rice.

MELT-IN-YOUR-MOUTH POT ROAST WITH BESAR & SPAETZLE

Pot roast is one of my favorite dishes—and served with spaetzle, what's not to love? The cinnamon, pepper, coriander, cumin, and hint of chile flakes bring this family favorite to a new level. If you want a little more heat, you can substitute berbere or baharat in place of the besar.

MAKES 4 SERVINGS

FOR THE BEEF:
3 pounds beef chuck pot roast, trimmed and patted dry
2 teaspoons ground besar
1 teaspoon kosher salt
1 tablespoon extra-virgin olive oil
1 large yellow onion, halved and cut into thin slices
3 cloves garlic, smashed

1 cup red wine
1 cup beef broth
3 large carrots, peeled and cut at an angle into 2-inch pieces
1 dried bay leaf
¼ cup heavy cream
Freshly ground black pepper

FOR THE SPAETZLE:
1¼ cups all-purpose flour
½ cup milk

2 large eggs, lightly beaten
¼ teaspoon kosher salt, plus more for seasoning
3 tablespoons butter, divided
Freshly ground black pepper
1 tablespoon finely chopped parsley

- Preheat the oven to 350 degrees F.

- Rub the roast with the besar and salt. In a 5½-quart Dutch oven, heat the olive oil over medium heat. Sear the roast on all sides. Add the onion and cook for 5 minutes. Add the garlic and cook briefly. Add the red wine and beef broth. Wrap the

continued

pot lid with a kitchen towel to prevent excess liquid from dripping back into the pot and toughening the meat. Secure the towel ends at the top and cover the pot.

• Place the pot on the center rack and bake for 1½ hours. Add the carrots and bay leaf and cook for 1 more hour, or until the meat shreds easily with a fork. Remove the bay leaf and discard. Transfer the roast to a plate or cutting board to rest. Swirl the cream into the pot. Season to taste with salt and pepper. Slice the meat, return to the pot, and cover to keep warm.

• To make the spaetzle, in a large bowl, whisk together the flour, milk, eggs, and salt until smooth.

• Bring a large pot of water to a boil. Using a spaetzle maker or large-holed potato ricer, squeeze 1 cup of the dough into the boiling water, using a metal spatula to scrape the dough off the spaetzle maker. After about 1 minute, the spaetzle will begin floating to the top; as this happens, skim the surface with a slotted spoon or strainer. Transfer to a large bowl and add 1 tablespoon of butter. Continue with the rest of the dough. Gently toss the spaetzle with the remaining 2 tablespoons butter and season with salt, pepper, and parsley.

• Serve the roast, carrots, and sauce over the spaetzle.

OVEN-ROASTED CHICKEN WITH HARISSA-HONEY GLAZE

A simple roasted chicken is enhanced when you add a great spice glaze. The robust flavors and the smoky heat of the harissa are well balanced by the honey. You can also try using berbere, besar, or za'atar instead. If you want to substitute Chinese five-spice, be sure to add 1 tablespoon tamarind paste to the mix.

MAKES 4 SERVINGS

FOR THE GLAZE:
¼ cup coarsely ground harissa
3 tablespoons extra-virgin olive oil
2 tablespoons honey
2 tablespoons freshly squeezed lemon juice
2 teaspoons lemon zest
½ teaspoon turmeric (optional)

FOR THE CHICKEN:
1 (2- to 3-pound) chicken
1 lemon, halved
1 teaspoon kosher salt
Freshly ground black pepper

FOR THE VEGETABLES:
¾ pound fingerling or baby potatoes, halved lengthwise
3 medium carrots, peeled and cut at an angle into 1-inch pieces
1 sweet yellow onion, halved and cut into ½-inch slices
2 tablespoons extra-virgin olive oil
1 teaspoon kosher salt
¼ teaspoon freshly ground black pepper
½ teaspoon sea salt

• To make the glaze, combine the harissa, olive oil, honey, lemon juice, lemon zest, and turmeric in a small bowl.

• Position a rack in the center of the oven and preheat the oven to 425 degrees F.

• Remove the bag of organs from the chicken cavity, along with any excess fat or stray pinfeathers. Rinse the chicken inside and out, then pat dry. Place the lemon halves inside the chicken. Using kitchen twine, tie the legs together and tuck the wing tips under the breasts. Rub the chicken with the kosher salt and pepper,

continued

then with the glaze (work it under the skin for extra flavor). Place the chicken in a 12-inch cast-iron skillet.

◆ In a large bowl, toss the potatoes, carrots, and onion with the olive oil, kosher salt, and pepper. Arrange around the base of the chicken.

◆ Bake the chicken for 30 minutes, baste with its own juices, and bake 30 minutes more. If the chicken is getting too much color, cover with foil, removing it for the last 5 minutes of cooking. It's done when the temperature in the thickest part of the thigh reaches 160 degrees F.

◆ Remove the chicken from the oven and sprinkle with the sea salt. Loosely cover with foil and let rest for 10 to 15 minutes. Remove the twine, slice the meat, and drizzle over more glaze. Serve with the roasted vegetables.

BERBERE SLOPPY JOES

———◆———

This version of sloppy joes with the berbere spice blend of allspice, fenugreek, ajwain, and chiles takes an old favorite and brings it to life with new flavors. Brioche buns and crispy lettuce add texture to this sandwich. Try this recipe using harissa or baharat in the meat instead of berbere to explore other seasonings.

MAKES 4 TO 5 SERVINGS

1 pound lean ground beef
1 tablespoon extra-virgin olive oil
1 cup diced yellow onion
1 clove garlic, minced
2 teaspoons ground berbere

1 cup water
1 (6-ounce) can tomato paste
1 tablespoon brown sugar
2 teaspoons Worcestershire sauce

Kosher salt and freshly ground black pepper
6 to 8 brioche buns, toasted
½ head iceberg lettuce, thinly sliced

- Brown the beef in a large skillet over medium-high heat. Drain any excess fat, then transfer the beef to a plate.

- Heat the olive oil in the same skillet over medium heat. Add the onion and sauté until translucent. Add the garlic and berbere and stir. Add the beef back to the skillet and stir to combine. Add the water, tomato paste, brown sugar, and Worcestershire and simmer for 10 minutes. Season to taste with salt and pepper.

- Serve on the brioche buns topped with shredded lettuce.

Sweets & Breads

Amanda's Cumin-Crusted
Cornbread 179

Nectarine Upside-Down Cake
with Cardamom Custard 181

Pumpkin Custard with
Kashmiri Garam Masala
and Maple Cream 184

Kashmiri Garam Masala–
Infused Chocolate Truffles 186

Moist Carrot Cake with
Kashmiri Garam Masala 189

Gingerbread Cake with Besar
and Caramel Pears 191

Kashmiri Curry Bread
Pudding with Spiced Nuts 193

Chinese Five-Spice
Shortbread Cookies 194

Peach Cobbler with Nutmeg,
Cardamom, and Cinnamon 197

Apple Galette with
Chinese Five-Spice 198

Lavender Pavlovas with
Blackberries and Cream 201

AMANDA'S CUMIN-CRUSTED CORNBREAD

—— ••◆•• ——

Amanda's husband married her for this cornbread. Its coarse texture, moist interior, and spectacular crust combine so perfectly, you'll fall in love with it too. You can vary the spices in the topping to suit any taste. Always preheat your skillet to ensure the best bottom crust.

MAKES 8 SERVINGS

1 cup coarse cornmeal or polenta

1 cup all-purpose flour

1½ teaspoons baking powder

½ teaspoon baking soda

½ teaspoon kosher salt

7 tablespoons butter, divided

2 large eggs

1½ cups buttermilk

½ teaspoon coarsely ground black pepper

½ teaspoon ground cumin

1 teaspoon sea salt

- Preheat the oven to 400 degrees F.

- In a large bowl, combine the cornmeal, flour, baking powder, baking soda, and kosher salt.

- In a small sauce pan, melt 6 tablespoons of the butter over medium heat.

- In a medium bowl, whisk together the eggs, buttermilk, and 4 tablespoons of the melted butter (make sure it has cooled slightly).

continued

- In a small bowl, whisk the remaining 2 tablespoons melted butter, black pepper, cumin, and sea salt; set aside.

- Put the remaining 1 teaspoon of butter in a 10-inch cast-iron skillet and set it in the hot oven to preheat. Meanwhile, pour the egg mixture into the cornmeal mixture and stir gently to combine. Do not overmix or the bread will toughen. When the butter is sizzling, carefully remove the pan from the oven. Swirl the butter to coat the bottom and add the batter. Jiggle the pan to even out the batter. Return to the oven and bake for 10 minutes.

- Drizzle the spiced butter evenly over the cornbread. Return to the oven and bake for 10 minutes more. The top of the cornbread should be lightly browned. If necessary, broil to finish the crust. The cornbread is best served right out of the oven, so cut into wedges and serve hot alongside Spicy Chili with Berbere (page 92) or with Brisket with Berbere and Whiskey Barbecue Sauce (page 165), or simply enjoy it as dessert with softened butter and a drizzle of honey.

NECTARINE UPSIDE-DOWN CAKE WITH CARDAMOM CUSTARD

This dessert is wonderful when nectarines are in season, but you can also use pears or plums when autumn comes around. We love the texture that cornmeal gives this cake. The star anise, cinnamon, and cloves complement the cake without overwhelming it.

MAKES 8 TO 10 SERVINGS

FOR THE CUSTARD:

2 cups milk

5 cardamom pods, gently cracked

6 egg yolks

¼ cup granulated sugar

FOR THE CAKE:

1⅓ cups all-purpose flour

¾ cup granulated sugar

1¾ teaspoons baking powder

¼ teaspoon freshly grated nutmeg

¼ teaspoon ground cinnamon

¼ teaspoon kosher salt

6 tablespoons unsalted butter, at room temperature, divided

1 cup milk

1 teaspoon pure vanilla extract

1 large egg

1 teaspoon lemon zest

⅓ cup dark brown sugar

2½ pounds nectarines or peaches, pitted and cut into 1-inch slices

- To prepare the custard, combine the milk and cardamom pods in a heavy-bottomed saucepan and bring to a simmer over medium heat. Cook just until small bubbles form around the edge of the pan, about 5 minutes. Remove from the heat and let steep for 10 minutes before discarding the cardamom.

- In a medium mixing bowl, whisk together the egg yolks and sugar until they thicken and turn a pale yellow color. Slowly pour in ½ cup of the infused milk, whisking constantly. Add the egg mixture into the remaining hot milk, stirring constantly with a wooden spoon. Place the saucepan over low heat and stir until the mixture thickens and coats the back of the spoon, about 5 to 7 minutes. Keep the heat low and don't cook for too long, as the custard will curdle.

continued

- Remove from the heat, strain the custard through a fine mesh sieve, and transfer to a mixing bowl. Place the bowl over a larger bowl filled with ice to cool the custard quickly. Bring to room temperature, stirring occasionally, then cover the custard directly with a piece of parchment or plastic wrap to prevent a film from forming on top. Store in the refrigerator for up to 3 days.

- Preheat the oven to 375 degrees F.

- In a large bowl, sift the flour, sugar, baking powder, nutmeg, cinnamon, and salt. Add 3 tablespoons of the butter and work into the mixture with your hands. Stir in the milk and vanilla and mix until moist. Mix in the egg and lemon zest with an electric mixer for 1 minute. Set aside.

- Melt the remaining 3 tablespoons butter in a 10- to 12-inch cast-iron skillet over medium-low heat. Sprinkle the brown sugar evenly over the butter. Let the butter and sugar cook for 3 to 4 minutes. Arrange the nectarine slices in a circular pattern (they can overlap a bit), starting from the outside and repeating until the center is reached.

- With a spatula, spread the batter as evenly as possible over the nectarines. Bake for about 40 minutes, or until the cake is dark golden-brown and a toothpick inserted in the center comes out clean. Let the cake cool in the pan on a wire rack for 15 minutes. Run a knife around the edge of the pan and invert the cake onto a serving plate. Serve warm or at room temperature.

PUMPKIN CUSTARD WITH KASHMIRI GARAM MASALA & MAPLE CREAM

———◆———

The toasted spice flavors of Kashmiri garam masala are amazing in this creamy pumpkin custard topped with maple cream. Crumbled ginger thin cookies form a bottom crust for a pleasing crunch. Baking the pies in jars is a whimsical way to serve them and a practical way to transport treats to a party or give as a gift.

MAKES 5 SERVINGS

FOR THE CRUST:

10 ginger wafers (we recommend Anna's Ginger Thins)

3 tablespoons unsalted butter

FOR THE CUSTARD:

2 large eggs

2 egg yolks

1 (15-ounce) can pumpkin puree

½ cup milk

¼ cup maple syrup

1 teaspoon ground Kashmiri garam masala

¼ teaspoon kosher salt

FOR THE CREAM:

1 cup heavy cream

2 tablespoons maple syrup

Freshly grated nutmeg, for garnish

◆ Preheat the oven to 350 degrees F.

◆ To make the crust, place the ginger wafers in a zippered bag and use a rolling pin to crush them. Transfer to a small bowl. Melt the butter in a small saucepan, then pour over the crumbs, tossing with a fork to mix well. Add 2 to 3 tablespoons of the buttered crumbs to the bottoms of 5 small canning jars, using the back of your hand to press down lightly. Set aside.

◆ To make the custard, whisk the eggs and egg yolks in a large bowl until combined. Stir in the pumpkin puree, milk, maple syrup, garam masala, and salt and combine thoroughly.

- Fill the jars two-thirds of the way with the custard mixture and place them in a roasting pan. Fill the pan with hot water until it comes halfway up the sides of the jars. Place the pan in the oven and bake for 50 to 55 minutes. Gently touch the top; if the custard is firm and doesn't jiggle in the center, it is done.

- To make the maple cream, whip the cream in a medium bowl until thickened. Add the maple syrup and continue to whip for a couple of minutes, or until soft peaks form. Top each custard with 2 tablespoons of the whipped cream and a dash of nutmeg.

KASHMIRI GARAM MASALA– INFUSED CHOCOLATE TRUFFLES

———•◆•———

Like all great pairings, Kashmiri garam masala and chocolate were meant to be together, and this recipe shows their relationship to its best advantage—pure and simple. You can make many different variations of the chocolate truffle using this recipe—we also enjoy Chinese five-spice and ras el hanout. If you want to dress them up even more and add a little spark of heat, try topping with flaked chiles like Aleppo or urfa biber.

MAKES 24 TO 28 TRUFFLES

8 ounces high-quality bittersweet or semi-sweet chocolate, coarsely chopped

½ cup heavy cream

2 tablespoons whole Kashmiri garam masala

1 cup sifted unsweet-ened cocoa powder

1 cup hazelnuts, lightly toasted and finely chopped

- Line a baking sheet with parchment paper; secure with tape.

- In a food processor, pulse the chocolate on and off until the pieces are the size of peas. You can also chop by hand into small pieces.

- In a heavy saucepan over low heat, warm the cream and garam masala until small bubbles start to form around the edges. Turn off the heat and allow the cream to steep for 15 minutes. Strain through a fine mesh sieve into a large bowl, discarding the spices. Add the cream back into the pot and bring just barely to a slight boil. Pour the cream into a clean large bowl. Add the chocolate pieces and press down with a spatula to submerge. Stir until the ganache is smooth. If not all of the pieces are melted, place the bowl in a hot water bath (being careful not to get any water in the ganache). Pour into a shallow metal or glass baking dish. Cover and refrigerate, stirring occasionally, until firm, about 2 hours.

- Using a small spoon, scoop out enough ganache to roll into 1-inch balls (use gloves if you don't want to get your hands messy). Place all the balls on the prepared baking sheet. On another baking sheet, sprinkle the cocoa and hazelnuts and roll the ganache balls around to coat as desired. Press on the nuts as you roll to get the truffles well coated.

- Place the truffles in mini cupcake or candy cups and serve, or wrap well and refrigerate for several days. The plain ganache will keep in the refrigerator in an airtight container for up to 1 month.

MOIST CARROT CAKE WITH KASHMIRI GARAM MASALA

Sometimes change is good—and in this case the flavor is what's new. Fans have deemed this the best carrot cake they've ever had! Serving a favorite dessert that is known and loved, like carrot cake, with a new twist is the joy of exploring with spice. Kashmiri garam masala lends roasted spice flavors of pepper, cardamom, and clove to this classic preparation, and the coconut oil adds wonderful moisture and a velvety texture.

MAKES ONE 9-INCH LAYER CAKE

FOR THE CAKE:

2 cups all-purpose flour

2 teaspoons baking soda

2 teaspoons baking powder

1 teaspoon kosher salt

2 tablespoons ground Kashmiri garam masala

4 large eggs

½ cup granulated sugar

½ cup brown sugar

1½ cups coconut oil, melted

3 cups grated carrots

1½ cups chopped walnuts or pecans, plus more for garnish

FOR THE FROSTING:

½ cup unsalted butter, at room temperature

8 ounces cream cheese, at room temperature

1 cup confectioners' sugar, sifted

2 teaspoons pure vanilla extract

- Preheat the oven to 350 degrees F. Line two 9-inch round cake pans with greased parchment paper.

- To make the cake, in a large bowl, combine the flour, baking soda, baking powder, salt, and garam masala.

- In a large bowl, whisk together the eggs and sugars. Add the melted coconut oil and whisk 1 minute more. Using a spatula, gently fold in the flour mixture. Fold in the carrots and walnuts. Fill the cake pans with equal portions of the batter and bake for 30 minutes, or until the tops of the cakes spring back to a light touch.

continued

Cool in the pans on a wire rack for 5 to 10 minutes, then remove the cakes from the pans and allow them to cool completely.

- To make the frosting, in a stand mixer fitted with the paddle attachment (or a large bowl with an electric mixer), beat together the butter and cream cheese until smooth. Add the confectioners' sugar and vanilla and continue mixing until the frosting is thick and smooth. You can adjust the consistency by adding a little milk if it is too stiff, or more sugar if it is too runny.

- We recommend a rustic presentation for this cake, so frost only between the layers and on top, leaving the beautiful colors and texture visible on the sides. Garnish with chopped nuts and serve.

GINGERBREAD CAKE
WITH BESAR & CARAMEL PEARS

———— ••• ————

This cake is not too sweet, so the addition of the caramel sauce and pears gives it the perfect balance. Top each serving with whipped cream or vanilla ice cream. You can also substitute Kashmiri garam masala or Chinese five-spice for the besar.

MAKES ONE 9-BY-13-INCH CAKE

FOR THE CAKE:
1½ cups water
⅔ cup molasses
1 teaspoon baking
    soda
½ cup unsalted butter,
    at room temperature
1 cup firmly packed
    light brown sugar
1 large egg

2½ cups all-purpose
    flour
2½ teaspoons baking
    powder
2 teaspoons ground
    besar
½ teaspoon kosher salt

FOR THE SAUCE:
1½ cups granulated
    sugar
⅓ cup water

1⅓ cups heavy cream

FOR THE PEARS:
5 ripe d'Anjou, Comice,
    or Bartlett pears,
    peeled, cored, and
    cut into ¼-inch slices
2 teaspoons freshly
    squeezed lemon
    juice
½ teaspoon fleur de
    sel or grey sea salt

• Preheat the oven to 350 degrees F. Butter the sides and bottom of a 9-by-13-inch baking pan.

• To make the cake, in a small pot, bring the water to a boil, then remove from the heat. Stir in the molasses and baking soda. Set aside to cool slightly.

• In the bowl of a stand mixer fitted with the paddle attachment (or in a large bowl using an electric mixer), cream the butter and sugar on high speed for about 2 minutes, or until light and fluffy. Add the egg and continue mixing. Sift together the flour, baking powder, besar, and salt. With the mixer at low speed, alternately add the dry ingredients and the molasses mixture a little at a time, mixing until combined. Pour into the prepared pan.

continued

- Bake for 35 to 40 minutes, or until a skewer inserted in the center comes out clean. Allow the cake to cool completely, then cut it into generous squares.

- To make the caramel sauce, in a medium saucepan over low heat, combine the sugar and water. Stir at first, then allow to caramelize without being disturbed for 5 to 10 minutes. Continue to cook without stirring until the mixture has reached about 350 degrees F, about 5 to 7 minutes. Gently swirl the pan if heat is not evenly distributed. Once you see a nice caramel color, remove from the heat. Add the cream quickly and return to the heat for 1 to 2 minutes stirring to incorporate. Set aside.

- In a large bowl, toss the pears with the lemon juice. Heat a cast-iron skillet over low heat. Add 2 tablespoons of the caramel sauce. Add the pears and gently stir to warm through, turning over once and cooking for about 5 minutes. Remove from the heat and set aside.

- Place a piece of cake on each plate, top with a few pears, and drizzle with caramel sauce. Sprinkle with a pinch of fleur de sel and serve.

KASHMIRI CURRY BREAD PUDDING WITH SPICED NUTS

———•••———

The warm aromatic spicing of Kashmiri curry pairs perfectly with this rich, moist bread pudding. The flavors infuse the entire dish, making each bite a delight, and the addition of spiced nuts adds a welcome crunch. This decadent dessert is wonderful served with brandy or a hot toddy on a winter's night.

MAKES 8 TO 10 SERVINGS

4 cups heavy cream
1 tablespoon ground
    Kashmiri curry
1 cup granulated sugar
4 large eggs

1 loaf brioche, crusts
    removed, cut into
    1-inch cubes
1 cup golden raisins
Sweetened whipped
    cream or ice cream,
    for serving

½ cup Irresistible
    Spiced Nuts
    (page 71), for
    serving

◆ Preheat the oven to 350 degrees F. Grease a 9-by-13-inch baking dish.

◆ In a medium saucepan, whisk together the heavy cream and curry. Bring to a slight boil, reduce the heat to low, and gently simmer for 5 minutes. Pour into a wide bowl and set aside to cool.

◆ In a large bowl, whisk together the sugar and eggs, then add the cooled cream. Put the cubed brioche and raisins in the bowl and, using a spatula, turn and press the bread into the liquid until it is absorbed.

◆ Scoop the mixture into the prepared baking dish and bake for about 30 minutes, or until a knife inserted into the pudding comes out clean and the bread is golden brown and crisp on top. Serve warm, with whipped cream or ice cream and a sprinkle of spiced nuts.

CHINESE FIVE-SPICE SHORTBREAD COOKIES

This is a great, versatile dough and can hold well, tightly wrapped, in the refrigerator. You can also freeze it for up to 1 month. Brush with egg white, roll in sugar, and bake. Try adding lavender and lemon to a batch—or even Kashmiri garam masala or ras el hanout in place of the Chinese five-spice!

MAKES 2 DOZEN COOKIES

1 cup unsalted butter, at room temperature
¾ cup granulated sugar
1 large egg
1 teaspoon pure vanilla extract

2¼ cups all-purpose flour
2 teaspoons grated orange zest
½ teaspoon ground Chinese five-spice

½ teaspoon kosher salt
1 egg white
½ cup coarse raw sugar (we recommend turbinado)

- In the bowl of a stand mixer fitted with the paddle attachment (or in a large bowl using an electric mixer) beat the butter and sugar together until pale, light, and fluffy. Add the egg and vanilla and mix until well blended. Add the flour, orange zest, Chinese five-spice, and salt and mix well.

- Divide the dough in half, shape each portion into a log, and place on a piece of parchment paper. Using the palms of your hands, roll the logs until they are about 1½ inches in diameter. Chill in the refrigerator for at least 1 hour.

- Preheat the oven to 375 degrees F.

- Brush the dough logs with egg white and roll in the raw sugar. Cut the logs into ¼-inch slices and place on a parchment-lined baking sheet. Bake for 12 to 15 minutes, or until the edges are golden brown. Cool on a wire rack. Serve with your favorite tea or a tall glass of milk.

PEACH COBBLER WITH NUTMEG, CARDAMOM & CINNAMON

This is our go-to peach cobbler recipe. August is the time of year when peaches are what we call "drip down your chin peaches". When they are really ripe and sweet, they are so juicy and delicious, and you can add less sugar. Serve with prosecco and vanilla ice cream—enjoy the wonderful tastes of summer!

MAKES 8 SERVINGS

FOR THE FILLING:
5 to 6 peaches, peeled, pitted, and cut into ½-inch slices, then halved (about 6 cups)
¼ cup granulated sugar
¼ cup brown sugar
2 tablespoons all-purpose flour

½ teaspoon ground cardamom
½ teaspoon ground cinnamon
¼ teaspoon ground nutmeg

FOR THE COBBLER:
1 cup all-purpose flour
¼ cup granulated sugar

1½ teaspoons baking powder
½ teaspoon baking soda
½ teaspoon kosher salt
1 cup heavy cream, whipped
¼ cup butter, melted
3 tablespoons brown sugar

- Preheat the oven to 375 degrees F. Lightly butter a 9-by-13-inch baking dish.

- To make the filling, in a large bowl, combine the peaches, sugars, flour, cardamom, cinnamon, and nutmeg and toss well.

- To make the cobbler, in a medium bowl, whisk together the flour, sugar, baking powder, baking soda, and salt. Fold in the whipped cream until it is incorporated but still has some volume. Add the peach filling to the prepared baking dish. Add the whipped topping by heaping spoonfuls, leaving about ½ to 1 inch around each lump of dough.

- Drizzle with the melted butter and sprinkle with brown sugar. Bake on the middle rack for 35 to 40 minutes, or until the cobbler is golden brown. Allow to cool for 5 to 10 minutes and then serve warm.

APPLE GALETTE
WITH CHINESE FIVE-SPICE

———— ◆◆ ————

This rustic freeform tart boasts a rich pastry studded with ground almonds and wrapped around a delicious center of apples and spice. It is a snap to make, and like so many of our favorite recipes—it is versatile. You can explore different types of apples and different blends of spice. We recommend using Honeycrisp for a sweet take, Braeburn for a balanced sweet and sour, or Granny Smith for tartness. Try using ras el hanout or besar for an even more exciting flavor.

MAKES 6 TO 8 SERVINGS

FOR THE PASTRY:
½ cup whole almonds
1½ cups all-purpose flour
3 teaspoons sugar
½ teaspoon kosher salt

10 tablespoons chilled
    unsalted butter, cut
    into pieces
½ cup ice water

FOR THE FILLING:
¼ cup maple syrup

1 teaspoon ground
    Chinese five-spice
½ teaspoon orange zest
3 crisp apples, peeled,
    cored, and cut into
    ¼-inch slices

◆ Preheat the oven to 400 degrees F.

◆ To make the pastry, put the almonds in a food processor and pulse to crack them into large pieces. Transfer to a heavy dry skillet and toast over medium heat until lightly browned. Remove from the pan and allow to cool. Return the almonds to the food processor and pulse sparingly until they resemble a coarse meal. Be careful not to overdo it—it will turn into almond butter! Add the flour, sugar, and salt to the food processor and pulse to mix. Add the butter and pulse in short bursts until the mixture forms into crumbs the size of peas. Add the ice water a few tablespoons at a time and pulse gently after each addition. After all the liquid has been added and the dough comes together, remove it from the food processor and form it into a large disc. Work quickly and don't handle the dough too much so that the butter stays cold. Wrap the dough in plastic wrap and refrigerate for 1 to 2 hours.

• In a large bowl, whisk together the maple syrup, Chinese five-spice, and orange zest. Add the apples and stir gently to coat.

• On a lightly floured surface, roll out the pastry into an oval about ⅛-inch thick. Transfer the pastry to a large parchment-lined baking sheet and arrange the apple slices, slightly overlapping, into concentric layers, leaving a 2 inch border around the edge. Fold the edges of the pastry back over the apples. The crust will pleat as you fold it, holding the apples neatly inside.

• Bake the galette for 40 to 45 minutes, or until the apples are tender and the crust is golden brown.

LAVENDER PAVLOVAS WITH BLACKBERRIES & CREAM

This is a very easy dessert to make—and so delectable! A pavlova is like a meringue but with a softer center, while still providing a nice crunch. We love the added flavor of laven-der with the blackberries. If you have superfine sugar, it will eliminate any graininess in the meringue, but regular sugar works too. It is important to add the sugar slowly, giving it time to be absorbed by the egg whites.

MAKES 10 MERINGUES

FOR THE PAVLOVAS:

1 teaspoon pure vanilla
   extract
1 teaspoon lemon juice
1 teaspoon cornstarch
1½ cups sugar
1 teaspoon ground
   dried lavender
6 large egg whites
¼ teaspoon salt

FOR THE SYRUP:

2 tablespoons water
¼ cup sugar
1 cup blackberries

FOR THE TOPPING:

2 cups whipping cream
1 tablespoon
   confectioners' sugar

1 teaspoon pure vanilla
   extract, or seeds
   scraped from
   1 vanilla bean
6 cups fresh blackber-
   ries or blueberries
2 tablespoons thinly
   sliced fresh mint
   leaves, for garnish

◆ Preheat the oven to 275 degrees F.

◆ Line 2 baking sheets with parchment paper. Using a small bowl about 4 inches in diameter, draw 6 circles on the parchment paper on each baking sheet.

◆ In a small bowl, whisk the vanilla, lemon juice, and cornstarch; set aside. In another small bowl, whisk together the sugar and lavender.

continued

- Combine the egg whites and salt in the bowl of a stand mixer fitted with the whisk attachment (or in a large bowl using an electric mixer). Beat until you achieve firm but not stiff peaks. Gradually add the lavender sugar 1 tablespoon at a time, beating well with each addition. Beat until the egg whites become shiny and thick. Pour in the vanilla mixture and gently fold into the egg whites.

- Spoon about ½ cup of the meringue onto the parchment in the center of each traced round. Using a small spoon, scoop out a spoonful of meringue, or make an indentation in the middle, for the berries and cream. Repeat with the rest of the meringue. Bake for 30 minutes, then turn off the oven, leaving the meringues to dry out and crisp up for another 20 minutes. Transfer to a wire rack to cool.

- To make the syrup, in a small saucepan over medium-low heat, stir together the water and sugar. Once the sugar has dissolved, add the blackberries. Heat for 3 to 4 minutes. Using a potato masher or fork, smash the blackberries. Cook 4 to 5 minutes more, or until the syrup starts to thicken. Remove from the heat, strain through a fine mesh sieve and discard the solids.

- To make the topping, add the cream, confectioners' sugar, and vanilla to a mixing bowl and whip with an electric mixer until thick, soft peaks form. Do not overwhip.

- To assemble, place a dollop of cream into the center of each meringue, top with 6 to 8 blackberries, drizzle with 1 to 2 tablespoons syrup, and garnish with a few strips of fresh mint.

Finishing Touches

Sunshine Vinaigrette
with Sumac and Aleppo 204

Apricot and Coriander
Salad Dressing 205

Berbere Ketchup 207

Wirtabel's Melon Chutney 208

Turkish Sweet Onion Jam
with Baharat 209

Ras el Hanout Spice Paste 211

Apple Butter with
Ras el Hanout 212

Classic Harissa Paste 213

Spiced Rhubarb-Orange
Marmalade 214

Chile-Infused Oil 217

Basic Curry Paste 218

Niter Kibbeh Spiced Butter 219

SUNSHINE VINAIGRETTE WITH SUMAC & ALEPPO

———◆———

This bright vinaigrette is bursting with flavor from every direction and makes a tangy topper for green and grain salads of all varieties.

MAKES 1½ CUPS

1 cup extra-virgin
   olive oil
⅓ cup white balsamic
   vinegar

2 tablespoons
   chopped fresh mint
1 tablespoon chopped
   parsley

1 tablespoon
   orange zest
1 tablespoon sumac
2 teaspoons Aleppo
   pepper

◆ Combine all the ingredients in a glass jar with a tight-fitting lid and shake well. The vinaigrette will keep in the refrigerator for about a month.

APRICOT & CORIANDER
SALAD DRESSING

———•◆•———

The combination of coriander and apricots is a true marriage of flavors. You can transform this dressing by adding a touch of curry. It makes a simple salad taste special.

MAKES ½ CUP

1 tablespoon shallot, finely diced

2 tablespoons rice wine vinegar

1 teaspoon Dijon mustard

2 teaspoons apricot preserves

¼ teaspoon ground coriander

4 tablespoons extra-virgin olive oil

2 to 3 tablespoons water

Kosher salt and freshly ground black pepper

- In a small mixing bowl, whisk together the shallot, vinegar, Dijon, apricot preserves, and coriander. Add the oil 1 tablespoon at a time, whisking well with each addition. Add the water to thin slightly. Season to taste with salt and pepper. The dressing will keep in the refrigerator for about 2 weeks.

BERBERE KETCHUP

⟶ •◆• ⟵

Your burgers and fries will taste better than ever with Berbere Ketchup. The mild heat and rich flavors of berbere blend together perfectly with the tomatoes. This version has a notable but mellow spice level, so add more berbere if you want to really feel the heat. And, to turn one sauce into two, just add a few extra ingredients to the ketchup and you've got cocktail sauce with a twist!

MAKES 4 CUPS

2 tablespoons extra-virgin olive oil
1 medium onion, diced
4 cloves garlic, minced
2 teaspoons ground berbere

1 (28-ounce) can crushed tomatoes
½ cup apple cider vinegar
¼ cup brown sugar

2 tablespoons tomato paste
1 tablespoon freshly squeezed lemon juice
2 teaspoons flake or kosher salt

- Heat the olive oil in a large saucepan over medium heat. Add the onion and garlic and sauté until softened. Sprinkle with the berbere and stir to coat. Cook 1 to 2 minutes, or until the berbere is fragrant.

- Add the tomatoes, vinegar, brown sugar, tomato paste, lemon juice, and salt and simmer the mixture, stirring occasionally, until it thickens to the consistency of ketchup. Check the seasoning and adjust if necessary.

- Cool the ketchup to room temperature. You can keep your ketchup chunky and rustic, or transfer it to a blender and process until it is uniform and smooth. Refrigerate in an airtight container; the ketchup will keep for up to 2 weeks.

> **NOTE:** You can easily adapt this ketchup into a wonderful cocktail sauce. Simply mix 1 cup of the Berbere Ketchup with ¼ cup prepared horseradish and 1 tablespoon freshly squeezed lemon juice. Serve with your favorite seafood as a dipping sauce.

WIRTABEL'S MELON CHUTNEY

———— ◦•◦ ————

This recipe was given to Julie's mother, Sharon Kramis, from the late Marion Cunning-
ham. She was a fantastic cook who befriended Sharon at James Beard's cooking classes in
Gearhart, Oregon, back in the 1970s. We wanted to share this amazing recipe with you
since the wonderful combination of whole spices and melons really make it unique.

MAKES SEVEN TO EIGHT 4-OUNCE JARS

1 large unripe or partially
   ripe honeydew or
   cantaloupe, cut into
   1-inch cubes (about
   6 cups)
4 to 5 pears or apples,
   peeled, cored, and

cut into ½-inch cubes
   (about 6 cups)
1 cup golden raisins
1 cup dark raisins
1 cup chopped peeled
   fresh ginger
4½ cups sugar

2 cups white distilled
   vinegar
1 teaspoon allspice berries
½ teaspoon whole cloves
2 (2-inch) cinnamon
   sticks

♦ Mix together the fruits, raisins, ginger, sugar, and vinegar in a large Dutch oven or
heavy saucepan. Combine the allspice, cloves, and cinnamon sticks in a piece of
cheesecloth, securing it with kitchen twine. Use a hammer to smash the spices a
couple of times so they release more flavor during cooking. Tuck the bag of spices
into the fruit. Bring the mixture to a boil over medium-high heat, stirring occasionally. Reduce the heat to medium-low and simmer for about 2 hours, or until
the chutney has thickened and darkened. Taste occasionally to check if it needs
more spice, sugar, or salt. When thick and dark, remove from the heat and discard
the spice bag.

♦ Put the hot chutney into clean, hot jars. Let cool to room temperature, then cover
and refrigerate. The chutney will keep for up to 1 month. For long-term preserv-
ing, ladle into sterilized jars and process according to manufacturer's instructions.

TURKISH SWEET ONION JAM WITH BAHARAT

The concentrated flavors of onion and spice make this jam a powerhouse. We've added a Turkish twist to the mix, with mint appearing alongside the baharat. It is easy to make and embellishes small plates and roasted meats with exotic flair. We like to keep some handy in the refrigerator to add to our sandwiches too.

MAKES 2 CUPS

3 tablespoons extra-virgin olive oil	2 tablespoons finely ground baharat, divided	¼ cup honey
4 large or 7 medium onions, halved and thinly sliced	2 teaspoons kosher salt, divided	¼ cup white wine vinegar
	¼ cup red wine	1 tablespoon chopped fresh mint

- Preheat the oven to 400 degrees F.

- Place a 5½-quart Dutch oven over medium heat. Add the olive oil and swirl around. Once hot, add the onion and stir to coat with oil. Sprinkle with 1 table-spoon of the baharat and 1 teaspoon of the salt, and stir to coat again. Cover the Dutch oven and place in the oven. Cook for 1 hour. Periodically remove the pan from the oven and stir the onions, scraping any brown bits from the bottom and sides of the pan. After 1 hour, place the lid slightly ajar. Cook for an additional 1 to 1½ hours, stirring and scraping the sides of the pan every 30 minutes, or until the onions are very soft and well browned.

continued

- Transfer the onions to a large cutting board and cool enough to handle. Chop the onions coarsely.

- In a large saucepan, combine the onions, wine, honey, vinegar, and the remaining tablespoon of baharat. Simmer over medium heat until the mixture has thickened to the consistency of jam, 5 to 10 minutes. Season to taste with the remaining salt and stir in the mint. Let the mixture sit at room temperature for at least 30 minutes before serving to allow the flavors to develop. This condiment can be stored in an airtight container in the refrigerator for up to 2 weeks.

RAS EL HANOUT SPICE PASTE

This highly adaptable paste brings flavor to any dish. Play around with all kinds of variations on this theme to create wet rubs for fish, poultry, red meat, and vegetables.

MAKES 1½ CUPS

2 tablespoons extra-virgin olive oil or clarified butter
1 medium onion, thinly sliced
2 cloves garlic, minced

1 tablespoon tomato paste
1 teaspoon honey
1 cup water
2 teaspoons ground ras el hanout

1 teaspoon all-purpose flour
¼ teaspoon kosher salt

- Heat the olive oil in a medium saucepan over medium heat. Add the onion and sauté until golden-brown. Add the garlic and sauté for 1 minute. Add the tomato paste, honey, water, ras el hanout, flour, and salt and simmer the mixture for 10 to 15 minutes, stirring often, or until the mixture starts to thicken. Season with additional salt.

- Refrigerate in an airtight container; the paste will keep for up to 2 weeks.

APPLE BUTTER
WITH RAS EL HANOUT

———◆———

If you don't have time to stand around and stir this apple butter, try the slow cooker method—or bake it at a very low temperature in a Dutch oven some rainy afternoon. It's so good that you can use it alone on toast. We also love making this with Kashmiri garam masala or Chinese five-spice. It's great with pork chops too!

MAKES 5 CUPS

12 to 14 sweet-tart apples, such as Granny Smith or	Pink Lady, cored and quartered 2 cups apple cider	1 cup sugar 2½ teaspoons ground ras el hanout

- In a medium saucepan over high heat, combine the apples and cider. Bring to a boil, then reduce the heat to low, and simmer until the mixture resembles applesauce. Pass through a food mill or sieve.

- In a 5½-quart Dutch oven or heavy pot, add the apple puree, sugar, and ras el hanout. Cook over medium-low heat, stirring often, for 1 to 2 hours, or until nice and thick. Ladle into sterilized jars and process according to manufacturer's instructions.

> NOTE: You can also put the pot into an oven set at 250 degrees F for about 3 hours. Alternatively, put the mixture into a slow cooker on low for at least 6 and up to 8 hours.

CLASSIC HARISSA PASTE

———•••———

We use this as a condiment for seafood or to spice up rice and grilled vegetables. You can add a variety of chiles from mild to hot, depending on your heat preference. Be sure to wear gloves if handling the hottest chiles.

MAKES 1 CUP

6 Thai or Fresno chiles, stems trimmed and roughly chopped

1 red bell pepper, cored, seeded, and finely chopped

4 cloves garlic, finely chopped

6 tablespoons distilled white vinegar

3 tablespoons brown sugar

2 teaspoons freshly squeezed lemon juice

2 teaspoons ground harissa

1 teaspoon kosher salt

• In a large heavy-bottomed saucepan, add all the ingredients and bring to a boil over medium-high heat. Reduce the heat to low and simmer for 10 minutes, or until some of the liquid has been absorbed. Let cool to room temperature.

• Transfer the mixture to a blender and blend until mostly smooth (some chunks are okay). Transfer to an airtight container and store in the refrigerator for up to 3 weeks.

SPICED RHUBARB-ORANGE MARMALADE

———◆◆◆———

This marmalade makes a great gift, and we love putting it on ice cream or toast. It's also excellent served with a sheep's milk cheese such as Petit Basque, a Tomme de Savoie, or any triple cream cheese.

MAKES 6 TO 7 PINTS

3 oranges

2 large lemons

2 pounds rhubarb, coarsely chopped

3 star anise

1 cinnamon stick

2 cloves

7½ cups sugar

- Prepare the citrus as follows: Using a zester or Microplane, grate the zest of 1 orange and then juice the orange (you should have about ¼ cup juice). Peel and section the other 2 oranges. Grate the zest of 1 lemon and juice the lemon (you should have about ¼ cup juice). Peel, seed, and section the other lemon.

- Combine the rhubarb, orange juice, lemon juice, star anise, cinnamon, and cloves in an enameled or stainless steel saucepan. Bring to a boil over medium-high heat. Cover, reduce the heat to low, and simmer for about 1 hour, or until the rhubarb is soft. Using a fork, remove the spices and discard. Stir in the sugar, increase the heat to high, and boil rapidly, stirring constantly, for about 5 minutes, or until the mixture is translucent and lightly holds its shape in a spoon. Turn off the heat and stir in the orange and lemon sections and zests. Stir occasionally until the marmalade cools to room temperature. Ladle into sterilized jars and process according to manufacturer's instructions.

CHILE-INFUSED OIL

Infusing chiles in oil is an incredibly easy process and offers the perfect method to evenly distribute chile flavors throughout a dish. This recipe uses Aleppo chile flakes, which are mild, but any chile flakes or whole pods can be used. If you want more intense heat, try pequin chiles.

MAKES 1½ CUPS

1½ cups avocado or light olive oil
½ cup Aleppo chile flakes
¼ cup sesame oil

- In a medium saucepan over low heat, combine the avocado oil and chile flakes and bring to 250 degrees F. Continue cooking at this temperature for 10 minutes, then remove from the heat. Stir in the sesame oil. Cover and allow the mixture to cool and infuse overnight.

- At this point, you can transfer the oil to a clean bottle and use it as is, or strain the oil to remove the chile flakes. If you choose to strain it, warm the oil back up first for easier straining. Use the oil pure and simple, or add dried chile pods to the bottle for decoration—and more heat!

BASIC CURRY PASTE

———◆———

This is another great base that will brighten any dish. You can add a little of this paste at the beginning of making a soup or stew, or for sautéing vegetables. Alternatively, rub it on chicken or fish before roasting.

MAKES ½ CUP

5 dried hot red chiles (or more to increase heat), seeded and finely chopped

1 shallot, finely chopped

2 cloves garlic, smashed

3 tablespoons ground tikka masala, poudre de Colombo, or Kashmiri curry

1 tablespoon tomato paste

1 tablespoon grated peeled fresh ginger

2 teaspoons lemongrass paste

1 tablespoon honey

½ teaspoon kosher salt

◆ Put all the ingredients into a large mortar and pestle; smash the pestle up and down and then in a circular motion until you have a nice paste. Alternatively, you can use a blender, but add a few tablespoons of canola oil or water to help process the mixture. Store in an airtight container in the refrigerator for up to 6 weeks.

NITER KIBBEH SPICED BUTTER

Spiced butter originated in Ethiopia, and everyone has their own version, but this is the one we like best. We also like to use other spice blends like Kashmiri curry or tikka masala. Try it instead of clarified butter with freshly cracked crab, lobster, or prawns!

MAKES 1 CUP

2 pounds unsalted butter, cut into small pieces

1 small onion, coarsely chopped

3 tablespoons finely chopped garlic

3 tablespoons finely chopped peeled fresh ginger

3 cardamom pods, slightly crushed, or 3 pinches of cardamom seeds

1 (1-inch) cinnamon stick

1 whole clove

1½ teaspoons ground turmeric

* In a heavy 4- to 5-quart saucepan, heat the butter over medium heat, stirring it with a spoon to melt it slowly and completely without letting it brown. Increase the heat and bring the butter to a boil. When the surface is completely covered with white foam, stir in the onion, garlic, ginger, cardamom, cinnamon, clove, and turmeric. Reduce the heat to low and simmer uncovered and undisturbed for about 45 minutes, or until all of the milk solids on the bottom of the pan are golden brown and the butter on top is transparent.

* Line a fine mesh sieve with several layers of dampened cheesecloth. Set it over a bowl, then slowly pour the spiced butter through the strainer. Discard the solids; if there are any solids left in the butter, strain it again to prevent it from becoming rancid. Pour the butter into a clean jar, cover tightly, and refrigerate. It will solidify when chilled and can be kept safely, even at room temperature, for 2 to 3 months.

Index

Note: Photographs are indicated by *italics*.

A

ajwain seed, 11, *27*, 28, *46*, 48, 118
Aleppo pepper. *See* pepper, Aleppo
allspice, 11, *24*, 25, *26*, 28, *47*, 48, 208
anise seed, 12, *47*, 48, *50*, 52
appetizers, 57–76
Apple and Crimson Beet Soup with Za'atar Cream, 83–84
Apple Butter with Ras el Hanout, 212
Apple Galette with Chinese Five-Spice, 198–199
Apricot and Coriander Salad Dressing, 205
Arugula and Urfa Biber, Summer Tomato Salad with, *102*, 103–104

B

Baharat
    Braised Beef Short Ribs with Caramelized Onions and Baharat, *160*, 161–162
    Irresistible Spiced Nuts, 71
    Picadillo Peppers with Baharat, 61–62
    recipe for, *24*, 25
    Seared Rib-Eye Steak with Baharat, *150*, 151–152
    Turkish Sweet Onion Jam with Baharat, 209–210
Barbecue Sauce, Brisket with Berbere and Whiskey, 165
Barbecue Sauce, Pork Ribs with Chinese Five-Spice and, 155–157, *156*
bay leaf, 12
beef. *See* meat and poultry
Beet and Apple Soup with Za'atar Cream, Crimson, 83–84

Beet Salad with Watercress and Dukkah Goat Cheese, Roasted, *98*, 99–100
Berbere
    Berbere Ketchup, *206*, 207
    Berbere Ketchup, Lollapalooza Lamb Sliders with, 63–65, *64*
    Berbere Sloppy Joes, 176
    Brisket with Berbere and Whiskey Barbecue Sauce, 165
    Niter Kibbeh Spiced Butter, 219
    Pan-Fried Sole with Berbere and Lemon Butter, 135–136
    recipe for, *26–27*, 28
    Spicy Chili with Berbere, 92
Besar
    Besar Shrimp and Pineapple Skewers, *66*, 67–68
    Gingerbread Cake with Besar and Caramel Pears, 191–192
    Golden Butternut Squash Soup with Besar, 85–87, *86*
    Maple-Glazed Pork Chops with Besar, 153–154
    Melt-in-Your-Mouth Pot Roast with Besar and Spaetzle, 171–172
    recipe for, 29, *30*
    Sausage, White Bean, and Kale Soup with Besar, 89
Blackberries and Cream, Lavender Pavlovas with, *200*, 201–202
black peppercorns. *See* peppercorns, black
breads and bread dishes
    Amanda's Cumin-Crusted Cornbread, *178*, 179–180
    Kashmiri Curry Bread Pudding with Spiced Nuts, 193
    Pogacha Flatbread with Sea Salt and Dukkah, *58*, 59–60
    Vegetable Bread Salad with Za'atar, 107–108
Broccoli with Lemon and Harissa, Crisp Oven-Roasted, 101
Bubble and Squeak with Poudre de Colombo, 105–106

Butternut Squash Soup with Besar, Golden, 85–87, *86*
butters
    Apple Butter with Ras el Hanout, 212
    infusing, basic tips for, 8
    Lemon Butter, Pan-Fried Sole with Berbere and, 135–136
    Niter Kibbeh Spiced Butter, 219

C

caraway seed, 12, *42*, 43, *47*, 48
cardamom
    about, 12
    Baharat, *24*, 25
    Berbere, *26*, 28
    infusions, tips for, 8
    Kashmiri Curry, *33*, 35
    Kashmiri Garam Masala, 44, *45*
    Nectarine Upside-Down Cake with Cardamom Custard, 181–183, *182*
    Niter Kibbeh Spiced Butter, 219
    Peach Cobbler with Nutmeg, Cardamom, and Cinnamon, *196*, 197
    Potato and Spinach Roll-Ups with Poudre de Colombo; variation, 120
    Ras el Hanout, *46*, 48
    shelf life, 4
    Tikka Masala, *36*, 39
    toasting, tips for, 6
Carrot Cake with Kashmiri Garam Masala, Moist, *188*, 189–190
Cauliflower and Leek Soup with Tikka Masala, Creamy, 88
cayenne pepper, 13, *27*, 28, *37*, 39, *42*, 43
chamomile flowers, 13, *47*, 48
chicken. *See* poultry
chile, guajillo, 14, 29, *30*, *33*, 35, *36*, 39, *42*, 43
chiles
    about, 3
    Basic Curry Paste, 218

Chile-Infused Oil, *216*, 217
chile powder, about, 29
Classic Harissa Paste, 213
types of, 13–15
chiles, pequin, 14, 28, *42*, 43
Chili-Garlic Sauce, Chinese
Five-Spice Chicken Wings with,
75–76
Chili with Berbere, Spicy, 92
Chinese Five-Spice
Apple Galette with Chinese
Five-Spice, 198–199
Chinese Five-Spice Chicken
Wings with Chili-Garlic
Sauce, 75–76
Chinese Five-Spice Shortbread
Cookies, 194, *195*
Grilled Steak Salad with Chinese
Five-Spice, 166–167
Pork Ribs with Chinese Five-
Spice and Barbecue Sauce,
155–157, *156*
recipe for, *31*, 32
Chocolate Truffles, Kashmiri Garam
Masala–Infused, 186–187
Chowder with Chanterelles, Bacon,
and Za'atar, Corn, 81–82
Chutney, Wirtabel's Melon, 208
cinnamon
about, 15
Baharat, *24*, 25
Berbere, *27*, 28
Besar, 29, *30*
Chinese Five-Spice, *31*, 32
Harissa, *42*, 43
infusions, tips for, 8
Kashmiri Curry, *33*, 35
Kashmiri Garam Masala, 44, *45*
Nectarine Upside-Down Cake
with Cardamom Custard,
181–183, *182*
Niter Kibbeh Spiced Butter, 219
Peach Cobbler with Nutmeg,
Cardamom, and Cinnamon,
196, 197
Ras el Hanout, *46*, 48
Spiced Rhubarb-Orange
Marmalade, 214, *215*
Tikka Masala, *37*, 39
toasting, tips for, 6
Udon Noodle Bowl with Prawns
In Star Anise Broth, *90*, 91
Wirtabel's Melon Chutney, 208
clams. *See* shellfish and seafood

cloves, 5–6, 8, 16
Cobbler with Nutmeg, Cardamom,
and Cinnamon, Peach, *196*, 197
cocktail sauce, *206*, 207
Cod with Harissa-Garlic Sauce,
Steamed True, 125–126
condiments, 203–219
conversions, 224–225
Cookies, Chinese Five-Spice
Shortbread, 194, *195*
coriander seed, 6, 16
Cornbread, Amanda's Cumin-
Crusted, *178*, 179–180
Corn Chowder with Chanterelles,
Bacon, and Za'atar, 81–82
Crab Melts with Kashmiri Curry,
Dungeness, *132*, 133–134
Crostini with Dukkah-Encrusted
Goat Cheese and Roasted
Tomatoes, 69–70
cumin seed, 6, 16
curries
about, 32, 35
Baked Chicken with Tikka
Masala Sauce, *168*, 169–170
Basic Curry Paste, 218
Besar Shrimp and Pineapple
Skewers; variation, *66*, 68
Bubble and Squeak with Poudre
de Colombo, 105–106
Coconut-Steamed Mussels with
Tikka Masala, 137
Creamy Cauliflower and Leek
Soup with Tikka Masala, 88
Dungeness Crab Melts with
Kashmiri Curry, *132*,
133–134
Kashmiri Curry, *33*, 35
Kashmiri Curry Bread Pudding
with Spiced Nuts, 193
Parsnip and Potato Soup with
Poudre de Colombo, 93
Potato and Spinach Roll-Ups
with Poudre de Colombo,
119–120
Poudre de Colombo, *34*, 38
Quinoa with Grilled Vegetables
and Kashmiri Dressing,
112–113
regional variations, 38
Skillet Prawns with Poudre de
Colombo, 138–139
Tikka Masala, *36–37*, 39

Custard, Nectarine Upside-Down
Cake with Cardamom, 181–183,
182
Custard with Kashmiri Garam Masala and Maple Cream, Pumpkin,
184–185

D
desserts and breads, 177–202
dill weed, 16, *49*, 51, 127–129, *128*
dry rubs, 7
See also meat and poultry
Dukkah
Crostini with Dukkah-Encrusted
Goat Cheese and Roasted
Tomatoes, 69–70
Crusted Rack of Lamb with
Syrian Za'atar, 163–164
Dukkah-Encrusted Seared
Scallops, *122*, 123–124
Niter Kibbeh Spiced Butter, 219
Pogacha Flatbread with Sea Salt
and Dukkah, *58*, 59–60
Pork Tenderloin with Ras el
Hanout and Urfa Biber Sweet
Potatoes, 158–159
recipe for, *40*, 41
Roasted Beet Salad with
Watercress and Dukkah Goat
Cheese, *98*, 99–100

E
Eggplant with Ras el Hanout,
Honey-Glazed, 109–111, *110*

F
fennel bulb
Corn Chowder with Chante-
relles, Bacon, and Za'atar,
81–82
Oyster Po' Boys with Harissa and
Muffuletta, *140*, 141–142
Pan-Roasted Halibut with Kash-
miri Garam Masala Glaze,
143–144
Skillet Prawns with Poudre de
Colombo, 138–139
fennel seed
about, 16–17
Besar, 29, *30*
Chinese Five-Spice, *31*, 32
Five-Seed Roasted Potatoes, 118

Kashmiri Curry, *33*, 35
Skillet Prawns with Poudre de
 Colombo, 138–139
fenugreek seed
 about, 17
 Berbere, *26*, 28
 Poudre de Colombo, *34*, 38
 Ras el Hanout, *47*, 48
 Tikka Masala, *37*, 39
fish. *See* shellfish and seafood
Fisherman's Stew with Harissa, *94*,
 95–96
Flatbread with Sea Salt and Dukkah,
 Pogacha, *58*, 59–60
Fries with Lemon-Pepper Aioli,
 Za'atar, *72*, 73–74

G

Galette with Chinese Five-Spice,
 Apple, 198–199
Garam Masala. *See* Kashmiri Garam
 Masala
garlic, 17, *27*, 28, *36*, 39, *42*, 43
Gazpacho with Urfa Biber,
 Heirloom Tomato, *78*, 79–80
ginger
 about, 17
 Baked Chicken with Tikka
  Masala Sauce, *168*, 169–170
 Basic Curry Paste, 218
 Berbere, *26*, 28
 Coconut-Steamed Mussels with
  Tikka Masala, 137
 Golden Butternut Squash Soup
  with Besar, 85–87, *86*
 Grilled Steak Salad with Chinese
  Five-Spice, 166–167
 Niter Kibbeh Spiced Butter, 219
 Pan-Roasted Halibut with
  Kashmiri Garam Masala
  Glaze, 143–144
 Pork Ribs with Chinese Five-
  Spice and Barbecue Sauce,
  155–157, *156*
 Potato and Spinach Roll-Ups
  with Poudre de Colombo,
  119–120
 Ras el Hanout, *47*, 48
 Tikka Masala, *37*, 39
 Udon Noodle Bowl with Prawns
  In Star Anise Broth, *90*, 91
 Wirtabel's Melon Chutney, 208
Gingerbread Cake with Besar and
 Caramel Pears, 191–192

glossary of spices, 11–22
grains of paradise, 17, *47*, 48
grinding spices, 5–6
Grits, Spicy Shrimp and, 147–148
guajillo chile. *See* chile, guajillo

H

Halibut Poached in Olive Oil with
 Saffron, 130, *131*
Halibut with Kashmiri Garam
 Masala Glaze, Pan-Roasted,
 143–144
ham. *See* pork and ham
Harissa
 Classic Harissa Paste, 213
 Crisp Oven-Roasted Broccoli
  with Lemon and Harissa, 101
 Fisherman's Stew with Harissa,
  94, 95–96
 Oven-Roasted Chicken with
  Harissa-Honey Glaze,
  173–175, *174*
 Oyster Po' Boys with Harissa and
  Muffuletta, *140*, 141–142
 recipe for, *42*, 43
 Shellfish Paella with Harissa and
  Urfa Biber, 145–146
 Spicy Shrimp and Grits, 147–148
 Steamed True Cod with Harissa-
  Garlic Sauce, 125–126
herb, definition of, 3
Honey-Glazed Eggplant with Ras el
 Hanout, 109–111, *110*
Honey-Harissa Glaze, Oven-Roasted
 Chicken with, 173–175, *174*
Hungarian paprika. *See* paprika,
 Hungarian

I

Infused Oil, Chile-, *216*, 217
infusions, spice, 8
Israeli Za'atar, *49*, 51
 See also Za'atar

J

Jam with Baharat, Turkish Sweet
 Onion, 209–210
Jicama and Watermelon Salad with
 Sumac, Crispy, 114, *115*

K

Kale, Sausage, and White Bean Soup
 with Besar, 89
Kale Tabbouleh with Pomegranate
 Seeds and Ras el Hanout
 Dressing, *116*, 117
Kashmiri Curry
 Basic Curry Paste, 218
 Besar Shrimp and Pineapple
  Skewers; variation, *66*, 68
 Dungeness Crab Melts with
  Kashmiri Curry, *132*,
  133–134
 Kashmiri Curry Bread Pudding
  with Spiced Nuts, 193
 Quinoa with Grilled Vegetables
  and Kashmiri Dressing,
  112–113
 recipe for, *33*, 35
Kashmiri Garam Masala
 Kashmiri Garam Masala–Infused
  Chocolate Truffles, 186–187
 Lollapalooza Lamb Sliders with
  Berbere Ketchup, 63–65, *64*
 Moist Carrot Cake with Kashmiri
  Garam Masala, *188*, 189–190
 Pan-Roasted Halibut with
  Kashmiri Garam Masala
  Glaze, 143–144
 Pumpkin Custard with Kashmiri
  Garam Masala and Maple
  Cream, 184–185
 recipe for, *44*, 45
Ketchup, Berbere, *206*, 207

L

lamb
 Crusted Rack of Lamb with
  Syrian Za'atar, 163–164
 Lollapalooza Lamb Sliders with
  Berbere Ketchup, 63–65, *64*
 Picadillo Peppers with Baharat,
  61–62
lavender flowers, 18, *47*, 48, *200*,
 201–202
long pepper, 18, *46*, 48

M

Maple-Glazed Pork Chops with
 Besar, 153–154
marjoram, 18, *40*, 41

Marmalade, Spiced Rhubarb-
   Orange, 214, *215*
measurement conversions, 224–225
meat and poultry, 7, 149–176
Melon Chutney, Wirtabel's, 208
mortar and pestle, 5–6, 7, *10*
mussels. *See* shellfish and seafood
mustard seed, brown or black,
   18–19, *34*, 38, *46*, 48, 118

N

Nectarine Upside-Down Cake with
   Cardamom Custard, 181–183,
   182
nigella seed, 19, *47*, 48, 118
Niter Kibbeh Spiced Butter, 219
Noodle Bowl with Prawns In Star
   Anise Broth, Udon, *90*, 91
nutmeg
   about, 19
   Baharat, *24*, 25
   Berbere, *26*, 28
   Kashmiri Garam Masala, 44, *45*
   Nectarine Upside-Down Cake
      with Cardamom Custard,
      181–183, *182*
   Peach Cobbler with Nutmeg,
      Cardamom, and Cinnamon,
      196, 197
   Ras el Hanout, *46*, 48
   shelf life, 4
   Tikka Masala, *36*, 39
Nuts, Irresistible Spiced, 71
Nuts, Kashmiri Curry Bread
   Pudding with Spiced, 193

O

Oil, Chile-Infused, *216*, 217
oils, infusing
Onions and Baharat, Braised Beef
   Short Ribs with Caramelized,
   160, 161–162
Onion Jam with Baharat, Turkish
   Sweet, 209–210
Orange-Rhubarb Marmalade,
   Spiced, 214, *215*
oregano, Turkish, 19, *49*, 51
Oyster Po' Boys with Harissa and
   Muffuletta, *140*, 141–142

P

Paella with Harissa and Urfa Biber,
   Shellfish, 145–146
paprika, Hungarian
   about, 14
   Baharat, *24*, 25
   Berbere, *26*, 28
   Besar Shrimp and Pineapple
      Skewers, *66*, 67–68
   Harissa, *42*, 43
   Ras el Hanout, *47*, 48
   Skillet Prawns with Poudre de
      Colombo, 138–139
   Tikka Masala, *36*, 39
paprika, shelf life of, 4
paprika, smoked
   about, 14
   Harissa, *42*, 43
   Oyster Po' Boys with Harissa and
      Muffuletta, *140*, 141–142
   Shellfish Paella with Harissa and
      Urfa Biber, 145–146
   Spicy Shrimp and Grits, 147–148
Parsnip and Potato Soup with
   Poudre de Colombo, 93
pastes, spice
   Basic Curry Paste, 218
   basic steps for making, 6–7
   Classic Harissa Paste, 213
   Ras el Hanout Spice Paste, 211
Pavlovas with Blackberries and
   Cream, Lavender, *200*, 201–202
Peach Cobbler with Nutmeg,
   Cardamom, and Cinnamon,
   196, 197
Pears, Gingerbread Cake with Besar
   and Caramel, 191–192
pepper, Aleppo
   about, 13
   Chile-Infused Oil, *216*, 217
   Sausage, White Bean, and Kale
      Soup with Besar, 89
   Spicy Shrimp and Grits, 147–148
   Sunshine Vinaigrette with Sumac
      and Aleppo, 204
pepper, cayenne. *See* cayenne pepper
pepper, long, 18, *46*, 48
peppercorns, black, 6, 19–20
peppercorns, Szechuan, 20, *31*, 32
Peppers with Baharat, Picadillo,
   61–62
pequin chile. *See* chiles, pequin
Po' Boys with Harissa and Muffuletta, Oyster, *140*, 141–142

Pogacha Flatbread with Sea Salt and
   Dukkah, *58*, 59–60
pork and ham
   dry rubs for, 7
   Golden Butternut Squash Soup
      with Besar, 85–87, *86*
   Maple-Glazed Pork Chops with
      Besar, 153–154
   Pork Ribs with Chinese Five-
      Spice and Barbecue Sauce,
      155–157, *156*
   Pork Tenderloin with Ras el
      Hanout and Urfa Biber Sweet
      Potatoes, 158–159
   Spicy Chili with Berbere, 92
Potato and Parsnip Soup with
   Poudre de Colombo, 93
Potato and Spinach Roll-Ups with
   Poudre de Colombo, 119–120
Potatoes, Five-Seed Roasted, 118
Poudre de Colombo
   Basic Curry Paste, 218
   Bubble and Squeak with Poudre
      de Colombo, 105–106
   Parsnip and Potato Soup with
      Poudre de Colombo, 93
   Potato and Spinach Roll-Ups
      with Poudre de Colombo,
      119–120
   recipe for, *34*, 38
   Skillet Prawns with Poudre de
      Colombo, 138–139
poultry
   Baked Chicken with Tikka
      Masala Sauce, *168*, 169–170
   Chinese Five-Spice Chicken
      Wings with Chili-Garlic
      Sauce, 75–76
   dry rubs for, 7
   Oven-Roasted Chicken with
      Harissa-Honey Glaze,
      173–175, *174*
prawns. *See* shellfish and seafood
Pumpkin Custard with Kashmiri
   Garam Masala and Maple Cream,
   184–185

Q

Quinoa with Grilled Vegetables and
   Kashmiri Dressing, 112–113

R

Ras el Hanout
Apple Butter with Ras el
Hanout, 212
Honey-Glazed Eggplant with Ras
el Hanout, 109–111, *110*
Kale Tabbouleh with Pomegran-
ate Seeds and Ras el Hanout
Dressing, *116*, 117
Pork Tenderloin with Ras el
Hanout and Urfa Biber Sweet
Potatoes, 158–159
Ras el Hanout Spice Paste, 211
recipe for, *46–47*, 48
Rhubarb-Orange Marmalade,
Spiced, 214, *215*
Roll-Ups with Poudre de Colombo,
Potato and Spinach, 119–120
rose petals, 20, *46*, 48

S

saffron
about, 20
Fisherman's Stew with Harissa,
94, 95–96
Halibut Poached in Olive Oil
with Saffron, 130, *131*
Shellfish Paella with Harissa and
Urfa Biber, 145–146
salad dressings
Apricot and Coriander Salad
Dressing, 205
Sunshine Vinaigrette with Sumac
and Aleppo, 204
vinegar infusions, 8
salads
Crispy Jicama and Watermelon
Salad with Sumac, 114, *115*
Grilled Steak Salad with Chinese
Five-Spice, 166–167
Kale Tabbouleh with Pomegran-
ate Seeds and Ras el Hanout
Dressing, *116*, 117
Roasted Beet Salad with
Watercress and Dukkah Goat
Cheese, *98*, 99–100
Summer Tomato Salad with
Arugula and Urfa Biber, *102*,
103–104
Vegetable Bread Salad with
Za'atar, 107–108

Salmon with Za'atar and
Sauce Gribiche, Grilled,
127–129, *128*
salts, types of, 22
sandwiches and roll-ups
Berbere Sloppy Joes, 176
Dungeness Crab Melts with
Kashmiri Curry, *132*,
133–134
Lollapalooza Lamb Sliders with
Berbere Ketchup, 63–65, *64*
Oyster Po' Boys with Harissa and
Muffuletta, *140*, 141–142
Potato and Spinach Roll-Ups
with Poudre de Colombo,
119–120
Sausage, White Bean, and Kale Soup
with Besar, 89
scallops. *See* shellfish and seafood
seasonal rotation of spice pantry, 4
seed spices. *See* coriander seed;
cumin seed; fenugreek seed;
nigella seed
shelf life of spices, 4
shellfish and seafood, 121–148
Besar Shrimp and Pineapple
Skewers, 66, *67*–68
Coconut-Steamed Mussels with
Tikka Masala, 137
Dukkah-Encrusted Seared
Scallops, *122*, 123–124
Dungeness Crab Melts with
Kashmiri Curry, *132*,
133–134
Fisherman's Stew with Harissa,
94, 95–96
Grilled Salmon with Za'atar
and Sauce Gribiche,
127–129, *128*
Halibut Poached in Olive Oil
with Saffron, 130, *131*
Oyster Po' Boys with Harissa and
Muffuletta, *140*, 141–142
Pan-Fried Sole with Berbere and
Lemon Butter, 135–136
Pan-Roasted Halibut with
Kashmiri Garam Masala
Glaze, 143–144
Shellfish Paella with Harissa and
Urfa Biber, 145–146
Skillet Prawns with Poudre de
Colombo, 138–139
Spicy Shrimp and Grits, 147–148

Steamed True Cod with Harissa-
Garlic Sauce, 125–126
Udon Noodle Bowl with Prawns
In Star Anise Broth, *90*, 91
Shortbread Cookies, Chinese Five-
Spice, 194, *195*
Sliders with Berbere Ketchup,
Lollapalooza Lamb, 63–65, *64*
Sloppy Joes, Berbere, 176
small bites, 57–76
smoked paprika. *See* paprika,
smoked
Sole with Berbere and Lemon
Butter, Pan-Fried, 135–136
soups and stews, 77–76
Spaetzle, Melt-in-Your-Mouth Pot
Roast with Besar and, 171–172
spice, definition of, 3
spice blends
Baharat, *24*, 25
Berbere, *26–27*, 28
Besar, 29, *30*
Chinese Five-Spice, *31*, 32
curries, about, 32, 35
dry rubs for meat, 7
Dukkah, *40*, 41
grinding and storage tips, 5
Harissa, *42*, 43
Israeli Za'atar, *49*, 51
Kashmiri Curry, *33*, 35
Kashmiri Garam Masala, 44, *45*
making pastes with, 6–7
Poudre de Colombo, *34*, 38
Ras el Hanout, *46–47*, 48
Syrian Za'atar, *50*, 52
Tikka Masala, *36–37*, 39
spice combinations, 9
Spiced Nuts, in Creamy Cauliflower
and Leek Soup with Tikka
Masala, 88
Spiced Nuts, Irresistible, 71
Spiced Nuts, Kashmiri Curry Bread
Pudding with, 193
spice glossary, 11–22
spice infusions, 8
spice pantry, 3–9
spice pastes. *See* pastes, spice
spice quality and freshness, 4, 9
spice rubs, 7
See also meat and poultry
spices, grinding, 5–6
spices, toasting, 6
spices, when to add, 9
spice terroir, 18

Spinach and Potato Roll-Ups with
    Poudre de Colombo, 119–120
spreads. *See* condiments
Squash Soup with Besar, Golden
    Butternut, 85–87, *86*
star anise
    about, 21
    Chinese Five-Spice, *31*, 32
    grinding, tips for, 5–6
    Halibut Poached in Olive Oil
        with Saffron, 130, *131*
    infusions, tips for, 8
    Spiced Rhubarb-Orange
        Marmalade, 214, *215*
    Udon Noodle Bowl with
        Prawns In Star Anise Broth,
        90, 91
storage of spices, 4
sumac
    about, 21
    Crispy Jicama and Watermelon
        Salad with Sumac, 114, *115*
    Crusted Rack of Lamb with
        Syrian Za'atar, 163–164
    Grilled Salmon with Za'atar
        and Sauce Gribiche,
        127–129, *128*
    Israeli Za'atar, *49*, 51
    Sunshine Vinaigrette with Sumac
        and Aleppo, 204
    Syrian Za'atar, *50*, 52
Sweet Potatoes, Pork Tenderloin
    with Ras el Hanout and Urfa
    Biber, 158–159
sweets and breads, 177–202
Syrian Za'atar, *50*, 52
    See also Za'atar
Szechuan peppercorns, 20, *31*, 32

T

Tabbouleh with Pomegranate Seeds
    and Ras el Hanout Dressing,
    Kale, *116*, 117
thyme, 21, *40*, 41, *49*, 51
Tikka Masala
    Baked Chicken with Tikka
        Masala Sauce, *168*, 169–170
    Basic Curry Paste, 218
    Besar Shrimp and Pineapple
        Skewers; variation, *66*, 68
    Coconut-Steamed Mussels with
        Tikka Masala, 137
    Creamy Cauliflower and Leek
        Soup with Tikka Masala, 88

recipe for, *36–37*, 39
toasting spices, 6
Tomatoes, Crostini with Dukkah-
    Encrusted Goat Cheese and
    Roasted, 69–70
Tomato Gazpacho with Urfa Biber,
    Heirloom, *78*, 79–80
Tomato Salad with Arugula and
    Urfa Biber, Summer, *102*,
    103–104
turmeric
    about, 21
    Berbere, *27*, 28
    Besar, 29, *30*
    Besar Shrimp and Pineapple
        Skewers; variation, *66*, 68
    Kashmiri Curry, *33*, 35
    Niter Kibbeh Spiced Butter, 219
    Oven-Roasted Chicken with
        Harissa-Honey Glaze,
        173–175, *174*
    Pan-Roasted Halibut with
        Kashmiri Garam Masala
        Glaze, 143–144
    Poudre de Colombo, *34*, 38
    Ras el Hanout, 48
    shelf life, 4
    Tikka Masala, *37*, 39

U

urfa biber
    about, 14–15
    Crostini with Dukkah-Encrusted
        Goat Cheese and Roasted
        Tomatoes, 69–70
    Heirloom Tomato Gazpacho
        with Urfa Biber, *78*, 79–80
    Pork Tenderloin with Ras el
        Hanout and Urfa Biber Sweet
        Potatoes, 158–159
    Sausage, White Bean, and Kale
        Soup with Besar, 89
    Shellfish Paella with Harissa and
        Urfa Biber, 145–146
    Spicy Shrimp and Grits, 147–148
    Summer Tomato Salad with
        Arugula and Urfa Biber, *102*,
        103–104

V

vanilla beans, 8, 21
vegetables and grains, 97–120

Vinaigrette with Sumac and Aleppo,
    Sunshine, 204
vinegar infusions, 8

W

Watermelon and Jicama Salad with
    Sumac, Crispy, 114, *115*
Whiskey Barbecue Sauce, Brisket
    with Berbere and, 165

Z

Za'atar
    about, 51
    Corn Chowder with Chante-
        relles, Bacon, and Za'atar,
        81–82
    Crimson Beet and Apple Soup
        with Za'atar Cream, 83–84
    Crusted Rack of Lamb with
        Syrian Za'atar, 163–164
    Grilled Salmon with Za'atar
        and Sauce Gribiche,
        127–129, *128*
    Israeli Za'atar, *49*, 51
    Syrian Za'atar, *50*, 52
    Vegetable Bread Salad with
        Za'atar, 107–108
    Za'atar Fries with Lemon-Pepper
        Aioli, *72*, 73–74

Conversions

VOLUME

UNITED STATES	METRIC	IMPERIAL
¼ tsp.	1.25 ml	
½ tsp.	2.5 ml	
1 tsp.	5 ml	
½ Tbsp.	7.5 ml	
1 Tbsp.	15 ml	
⅛ c.	30 ml	1 fl. oz.
¼ c.	60 ml	2 fl. oz.
⅓ c.	80 ml	2.5 fl. oz.
½ c.	125 ml	4 fl. oz.
1 c.	250 ml	8 fl. oz.
2 c. (1 pt.)	500 ml	16 fl. oz.
1 qt.	1 l	32 fl. oz.

LENGTH

UNITED STATES	METRIC
⅛ in.	3 mm
¼ in.	6 mm
½ in.	1.25 cm
1 in.	2.5 cm
1 ft.	30 cm

WEIGHT

AVOIRDUPOIS	METRIC
¼ oz.	7 g
½ oz.	15 g
1 oz.	30 g
2 oz.	60 g
3 oz.	90 g
4 oz.	115 g
5 oz.	150 g
6 oz.	175 g
7 oz.	200 g
8 oz. (½ lb.)	225 g
9 oz.	250 g
10 oz.	300 g
11 oz.	325 g
12 oz.	350 g
13 oz.	375 g
14 oz.	400 g
15 oz.	425 g
16 oz. (1 lb.)	450 g
1½ lb.	750 g
2 lb.	900 g
2¼ lb.	1 kg
3 lb.	1.4 kg
4 lb.	1.8 kg

TEMPERATURE

OVEN MARK	FAHRENHEIT	CELSIUS	GAS
Very cool	250–275	130–140	½–1
Cool	300	150	2
Warm	325	165	3
Moderate	350	175	4
Moderately hot	375	190	5
	400	200	6
Hot	425	220	7
	450	230	8
Very Hot	475	245	9

Our Spice Roads

ABOUT AMANDA

Botanist, Chemist, Spice Merchant, Cook

It is unlikely that anyone could have predicted my future as a spice merchant, but the signs were all there from the beginning. My interest in plants started at the ground level in childhood, with my hands in the dirt, always checking out the twigs and stems. This led to a degree in botany and organic chemistry, followed by several years in the medicinal herb industry. I have always studied the plant kingdom with infinite interest—in both the field and the lab.

One day, I turned left instead of right on the sidewalk and my nose led me into "the spice shop" on the Seattle waterfront. It was love at first sniff! I began spice hunting in earnest and the kitchen became my new research lab. That was over a decade ago, and I've never looked back. As the owner of World Spice Merchants, my passion for all things botanical has come full circle and I am pleased to share this glimpse into our world of spices with you! Visit us in Seattle, or online at WorldSpice.com.

ABOUT JULIE

Cookbook Author, Chef, Cooking Teacher, Mom

Not a day goes by when I am not thinking about food and different things I want to try. I have been cooking professionally for over twenty years now, and I co-authored *The Dutch Oven Cookbook*, *The Cast Iron Skillet Cookbook*, and *Cast Iron Skillet Big Flavors*. I am always cooking, shopping at the market, or in the kitchen, learning something new.

When I open the door and step inside World Spice Merchants, the aromas overwhelm me and draw me along the path of exploration. Large glass jars containing magic flavors line the walls. Labels with strange names invite curiosity. We hope to open a new world of flavors in your kitchen. Thanks for coming along.